My Visits to Heaven and Hell

by

Elizabeth Saidimu

My Visits to Heaven and Hell
Copyright © 2013, 2014, 2017 — by Elizabeth Saidimu
ALL RIGHTS RESERVED
No part of this book may be reproduced or transmitted in any form or by any means, electronic or mechanical, including photocopying, recording, or by any information retrieval system without the express permission of the author.

Unless otherwise noted, all Scripture quotations are from The Holy Bible, King James Version, public domain.

Disclaimer: The author believes that the advice presented here is sound, but readers should not hold her responsible for either the actions they take or the results of those actions. The information contained in this book might not be agreeable with everyone, as it emanates from the author's personal experience with God and His Holy Spirit. The reader must carefully investigate all aspects of any spiritual decision before committing him- or herself. The author obtained the information contained herein from her own personal experience with the Spirit of God and other sources she believes to be reliable, but she neither implies nor intends any guarantee of accuracy. The author is not in the business of giving spiritual, physical, or any other type of professional advice. Should the reader need such advice, he or she must seek services from a competent professional. The author particularly disclaims any liability, loss, or risk taken by individuals who directly or indirectly act on the information contained herein.

Elizabeth Saidimu
P.O. Box 61081-00200
Nairobi, Kenya, East Africa

Email: emsaidimu@yahoo.co.uk

ISBN 978-1-940461-19-9

Printed on demand in the US, the UK and Australia
For Worldwide Distribution

About the Author

Elizabeth Saidimu is the founder of Heaven Light Ministries International based in Nairobi, Kenya. She holds a Masters degree in Business Administration (MBA) and was a banker for twenty-eight years. She left formal employment when the Lord called her to serve Him on a full-time basis. This did not come as a surprise to her, since she had been in communication with Jesus on the issue for more than eleven years.

In this book, Elizabeth details how, over a period of three years, she travelled several times to both Heaven and Hell. Out of that travel and the training it provided her, the Lord asked her to write this book. This is not just a book written out of man's knowledge or understanding; it is a record of the experiences that she has had with Jesus.

The experiences and miracles that Elizabeth has had with the Lord are enormous. He communicates to her in different ways, just as He does with many other people. She was instructed by the Lord to take most of these messages to the nations of world. By the grace and favor of God, she has been hosted by many radio and television stations in Kenya and has also taken her message to other nations such as Malawi, Zambia and Tanzania.

After Elizabeth left her employment, the Lord sent a 63-year-old lady from the United States to come and bring her His anointing. This lady had never been to Africa and even her air ticket to Kenya was a miracle.

Elizabeth is married and is blessed with four children.

Dedication

I dedicate this book to the Lord Jesus Christ, the Creator of Heaven and Earth, who is the Beginning and the End. He is the only reason that I live. Glory be to His name.

Acknowledgments

First, I give magnificence, tribute and honor to our Lord Jesus Christ for giving me the information in this book and for helping me put it together.

Second, I express my heartfelt appreciation to my spiritual father, Pastor Jeremiah, who supported me through the tough moments when even close friends could not understand what I was going through.

I must thank my family, my loving husband, Mr. Robert and my beautiful angels — Gloria, Sylvia, Sheila, and Esther — for your understanding and support throughout my training by the Lord.

I am also very grateful to Priscilla and Lucy. Without them, this may not have been possible.

Finally, my sincere appreciation to all my friends and colleagues for being there for me.

Also my sincere appreciation to my adopted US "daughter," Jeanette Biggers.

May Almighty God bless all of you.

Contents

Foreword by Jeanette Biggers 11

Introduction 13

Preface: The Very Beginning 25

Chapter One: Some of the Lessons the Lord Taught Us 33
Chapter Two: Enter Priscilla 37
Chapter Three: The Powers of Darkness 41
Chapter Four: More Fighting with Satan and His Demons 57
Chapter Five: My First Trip to Hell 67
Chapter Six: The Twelve Basements of Hell 85
Chapter Seven: Messages from Jesus 107

Message No. 1: Confession and the Transferables 109
Message No. 2: A Study Guide 115
Message No. 3: I Do What I Hate 125
Message No. 4: Proof of Discipleship 131
Message No. 5: Faith Is Like a Muscle 137

Message No. 6: Financial Planning God's Way 143

Message No. 7: Confession and Forgiveness 151

Message No. 8: God Wants His Word to Work 155

Message No. 9: Praying in the Spirit 163

Message No. 10: Turning Your Challenge into Blessings . 187

Message No. 11: Tithing, Other Giving and Stewardship 193

Message No. 12: God's Nature Is to Bless 199

Message No. 13: Every Member Is a Ministry 203

Message No. 14: The Heavenly Network 209

Chapter Eight: Called to Full-Time Ministry 241

Ministry Contact Page 257

Foreword by Jeanette Biggers

I do not believe that it is by chance that you are reading this book. For some, it will answer questions that you have had but didn't know whom to ask or how. For the rest of you, the stories and testimonies will challenge and stretch you, as you learn how our heavenly Father has used Elizabeth Saidimu. It can truly be said that she has been used in ways that are rarely heard about in churches today.

While some testimonies may be difficult to fathom, I encourage you to learn from the ones you can comprehend and put the others on a spiritual shelf for later. The Lord may begin to open your understanding to another area of His Kingdom work. This will, in turn, enable you to see how great He really is and how the enemy of our soul is no match for Almighty God and His Son, Jesus Christ, our Savior.

Elizabeth and I have been good friends since the Lord, through an astonishing set of miraculous circumstances, caused our paths to cross. We have ministered together in Kenya, and I have stayed in her home. She is genuine in her love for the Lord and has been willing to do the sometimes unusual things the Lord has asked of her.

My Visits to Heaven and Hell

May the Lord bless you as you read and step into the adventures that have been a part of Elizabeth's life and ministry.

Jeanette Biggers
Ambassadors Of Heaven Ministries

Introduction

Through the pages of this book, I would like to share with you some of the experiences I have had with God in the recent past. All the experiences I relate here are from Jesus Christ. He asked me to put them into a book so that others can read and know some of the things that befall us and our people. In obedience to our Lord Jesus Christ, I narrate the experiences and, in so doing, I hope to stir you to allow Jesus to operate in your life. He is interested in every detail of your life. He knows everything about you, and He wants to make your life whole. It is for that reason that He came. He said:

> *I am come that they might have life, and that they might have it more abundantly.*   John 10:10

If you allow Him to operate in you, that you may decrease, so that He may increase in you, you will begin to see change in your life and that of your family.

For a period of not less than three years, Jesus Christ visited me in my home and trained me in several areas. (John 14:23: *"Jesus answered and said unto*

My Visits to Heaven and Hell

him, If a man love me, he will keep my words: and my Father will love him, and we will come unto him, and make our abode with him.") He taught me the Bible. We had Bible classes with Him for many hours. I say *we*, because sometimes the training was with my children, and sometimes it was only for me. In the process, the Lord took me to places on earth, to Heaven and to Hell. He shared with me many issues and principles that are very key to the life of a believer.

What I am about to share with you in this book is from the Lord Himself. It is my prayer that you will believe what I have put down and in the process that you will seek God in your own way, that He may be real to you as He has been to me and to many other people who have chosen to listen to His voice.

Many times, when we have read books written by those who have had a visitation from the Lord, we simply put them back on the shelf and forget them. I was also guilty of this, but after my experience, I am changed, and I know that Jesus Christ is Lord, and He visits with His people, for He is alive, walking on the face of the earth and talking.

As you know, those who are living talk. If you believe that Jesus is alive today, I am sure you will also agree with me that He also talks (see John 10:27). If Jesus Christ is the Head of your family or your life, then you must also recognize that heads talk. They talk when giving us instructions, encouragement, or even when rebuking us. Just as the head of a family talks and the head of any organization talks, we need to know that Jesus Christ will talk to His people, giving us instruction and encouragement and even rebuking us. He is talking today and will continue talking. People stop talking only when they die. Please take what I am saying in this book as serious as you can. I had never thought that I would be doing this in my whole life, but when Jesus Christ visits you, your life can never be the same again. I am urging you to take this information seriously. You never know, this could be the only way that Jesus Christ will gain access to you and change your life.

I was once a very difficult person with a lot of questions. I would never simply accept statements at face value. Someone had to convince me beyond a reasonable doubt about God and about the fact that He still talks. If you will open yourself to Jesus and let Him teach you, you will have no reason to continue the way you are. Jesus Christ asked me to put this information into a book, so that many people can read and know that He is indeed God, and He wants to be a Friend and help you to make your life better from this day forward.

The Bible is full of testimonies of people who walked with God and had such experiences. I can speak authoritatively because of what He has done in my life. Why don't you allow God to give you such an experience, as He did with the men and women of the Bible? Were those people we read about in the

My Visits to Heaven and Hell

Bible who walked and talked with God any different from you and me? The only difference may be that we have not allowed God to work in our lives as He would want to. It is my prayer that my experience will stir your faith, and that you will desire that Jesus visit you too. He said that He was not leaving us as orphans, but that he would ask His Father to give us a Counselor to be with us forever (see John 14:16). That is why He desires to walk with you, talk to you and give you directions while on this earth. He wants to make your life better, so that you can help others come to Him and do His number one job, which is winning souls.

I will now take you back to the training and visitations that I had with Jesus. He asked me to start a Bible study in my house, and I did. In that Bible study, I took those attending through the training the Lord had given me. Jesus had asked me to buy writing materials and place them on the table and told me that He would be giving me written messages for the Bible study. Every day He would write at least two large pages of teaching. These messages are still available in their original hand-written form and can be accessed by anyone who wishes. During these Bible studies, therefore, I would simply read through what the Lord had instructed me to train on.

Before He started doing these written messages, He visited me and asked me to start a fellowship at my place of work. As usual, I had excuses to make, just as the men and women whom God called in the Bible. A good example of this was Moses. He gave God many excuses as to why he could not go to the Pharaoh. Another example is Daniel, when God called him, and, of course, Jonah. I also had some excuses as to why I could not do it. I told the Lord that I would not know how to lead such a fellowship. To my thinking, I had many valid reasons why I couldn't do it. The most important was that I did not know the Bible, and I was still a young believer, and some of the people He was asking me to lead had been born-again for years. The Lord did not accept my excuses. He told me that He would be showing me where to read from the Bible and telling me what else to say. I battled with this mandate until I could no longer resist.

When I finally agreed to start the fellowship, something very strange started happening. The night prior to the fellowship, He would show me the people who would be attending in a dream and give me the right message for them. I would share with them in the dream, and the following morning, during the fellowship, the people I had seen in my dream would come, dressed in the same way that they had been dressed in my dream. They would sit in the same spot where they had sat in my dream. I would not start until the last person had arrived, since I knew who was to come and exactly where they would sit. This continued for two years. It's was after this that the Lord started giving me written messages, some of which I will include in the book.

My Visits to Heaven and Hell

Another experience I would like to share occurred when the Lord appeared in court on my behalf. A man called me at my work in the bank and told me that I was needed at the offices of the City Council, because there was a discharge of sewer water from my house to my neighbors. When I got to the offices, they confirmed that I had been charged with this offense, and I was arrested and escorted from the office by two City Council policemen at about 5:30 p.m. that day. They proceeded to demand a bribe of 20,000 Kenyan Shillings (Kshs.) to give me my freedom. I declined and told them that I was ready to go to court and defend myself. They quickly reduced the figure from 20,000 to 15,000, then to 10,000 and 5,000, and I refused their demands at every point. Finally, they went all the way down to just 2,000 Kenyan Shillings, but when I still refused, they got angry, locked my car, and made me march from the Nairobi City Hall to the Kamukunji Police Station to be book into jail.

When we got to the police station, these men told me to tell the officer who was to receive me that I had only had Kshs. 1,500 on me and see if he would release me. They suggested this amount because I had told them that I only had Kshs. 1,700, but I was not about to bribe anyone. They suggested that I use the difference, Kshs. 200, for transportation home because I would not be getting my car back until the following day.

They handed me over to a very rough police officer, telling him that he should help me, since I had only

Kshs. 1,500. The man was very clear that he would not do business for such a paltry sum. "One thousand five hundred only?" Little did he know that I was not going to give him any money at all.

I was locked up in a filthy cell together with dirty parking boys and girls, and hawkers, both men and women. After some time, we were separated, men in their own room and women in theirs. But it was a place you would not want to be, even for a few minutes. All dignity goes out the window, and you do as you are told, without asking any questions. From the time one enters this place, their name is changed to *"Mahabusu,"* literally "Convict."

My cellmates were very friendly and talked to one another about what had brought them to such a place. One of them was brought a small loaf of bread (400 grams) and a half-liter packet of milk, and this is what we all shared for dinner. She opened the bread and passed it around, and each one of us took a slice. She opened the packet of milk, and it was passed around, and we each took a sip.

The following morning I was taken to court, and when the men who had arrested me saw me, they knew that there was going to be a problem. One of them came to me, greeted me in a very friendly manner, and gave me some advice. He said that I should plead guilty, since my case was a very serious one. If I pleaded guilty, he said, I would be charged only Kshs. 30,000, but if I refused to plead guilty, I might end up paying Kshs. 300,000. I said to him, "If I plead guilty to a crime that I have not committed, what will I tell Jesus when we meet?" With this, the fellow got very confused and stopped attempting to persuade me to accept the charges.

My attorney was present when my case was called, and after the charges were read, the prosecutor noticed that there was a mistake in the way the charges were drawn up. He requested that the court be allowed to amend the charges. This meant that we would have to come back to court another day. In the end, what followed was a long drawn-out court case that lasted for three years. I was in court twice a month during that time. The first time for mention, and the second time for hearing. This proved to be a very expensive and painful process, considering that I was a banker and a holder of the keys to the strong room or safe. Every time I had to go to court I needed my boss to authorize my absence and another officer had to be allocated to take over my keys and responsibilities.

All of this time, I was out on a bail of Kshs. 50,000.

Once, after I had been transferred to our head office, I went to share God's Word in another department, and after I finished, I asked those who attended if they had any questions. This is something I do even today every time I share with people, even in a church setting. I always give them time to ask questions.

That day the people started asking questions, and this went on until the door leading into my office was closed for security purposes. It was now 8:30 a.m., and the doors would not open until 9:00. This meant then that I could not start work until then. When this happened, I casually said to the people I was sharing with that since I was doing God's work, He would have to take care of what I was expected to be doing.

We continued our conversation until 9:00 a.m., when the doors opened, and then I went back to my office.

Just as I was settling down to work, a lady from my attorney's office called. She asked me where I was. I told her that I was in the office. She said I should immediately go to the court house, as my attorney was waiting for me there. This statement really surprised me. When she said, "Go back to court," I thought something was wrong with her.

I asked her, "Well, was my case on today?"

"Yes," she answered, "and you are being waited for."

I left the office in a hurry, went to the court and found my attorney waiting outside. He approached me and asked, "Where did you go? I have been looking for you?"

I told him that I had not known the case was on that day. He said, "You did not what? I saw you in court early this morning."

I told him that he was mistaken. I had not been in court. He insisted that he had seen me and then, when my case was called, he realized that I had walked out and not come back. He told the magistrate he didn't know where I had gone and asked for some time to produce me, and it was granted.

The attorney now realized that he needed to prepare me to answer questions about where I had gone. At that moment, he did not want to discuss the point of my being in court or not, he said. He just wanted me to know that I would have to answer questions about my whereabouts. Then he reminded me that as an attorney he would be in trouble with the court if I started debating the issue of whether or not I had been there earlier. So, from that point forward, there could be no more discussion about my being in court or not. He was sure he had seen me and had reported that to the judge.

As the attorney was explaining all of this to me, the court clerk came by and asked me, "Elizabeth, *ulienda wapi* (Elizabeth, where did you go?)" This seemed to indicate that he, too, had seen me in court. I could not understand how the two of them could have confused me for someone else. I thought to myself, "At least by the way I was dressed you would think I was different from the person they thought was me."

The attorney said, "You are going to be asked where you were, and you should have a clear answer. You will have to tell the court where you had gone."

I told him that I had not been in court earlier. I had not even known that the case was on for that day. He said he could not take chances like this, so he suggested, "Tell the court that you went to the washroom, you felt dizzy and wanted some fresh air, or you have a running stomach." As he was saying these things, I kept saying to God, "Lord, I refused to lie in the beginning, and because of that, I have been in court for three years now. Please, God, help me not to lie."

I asked my attorney, "Must that question be asked?"

He said, "Yes, and the answer must come from you."

Before we could agree on anything, the clerk of court came and said that it was our turn. I walked in and stood at the dock and waited for that question and trusted that God would help me not to speak a lie.

The magistrate addressed my attorney, "So Mr. Kisena (not his real name), where did you say your client was?" and he repeated what he had said before, that I had gone out for a while. Then, without further questions, we were asked to continue with our defense.

That day I left the courtroom wondering what had happened to those two men. They had seen me appearing in court over nearly three years, and yet they could still confuse me for another person? This bothered me. That night the Lord told me that He had been the one who had appeared in court, and so the two men were not lying. They actually saw me.

My Visits to Heaven and Hell

On many other occasions the Lord has appeared as me. He has even used my cell phone to make calls, but that is another story for another time.

Preface:

The Very Beginning

The Bible study I started in my home took place between 1:00 and 4:00 p.m. each Sunday afternoon. By the third week of our meetings, at around midnight on Friday night, the Lord asked me to call one of our members and ask her what time she would be arriving on Sunday. Since the meetings were scheduled to start at 1:00, we were all expected to be there and be seated by 12:45. When I asked the woman what time I should expect her, she said she would be there by 8:00 in the morning. When she said that, Jesus Christ agreed that indeed that was the time He expected her and her family to come.

The following evening, Saturday, Jesus Christ allowed us to go to bed early. Usually we would go to bed between 3:00 and 4:00 a.m. There were days when the training would continue until morning. I asked Him how we would manage, but He told me that He is a God of many plans. Usually, on Sundays, we would

My Visits to Heaven and Hell

wake up at 6:00 and prepare enough food for lunch for the whole group and enough for supper for our own family. The answer He gave me surprised all of us. He started by informing us of the time we should wake up the following day, Sunday. He said that we should all wake up at 5:00 a.m. He went on to allocate duties to each one of us.

The Lord started with my baby, Esther, who was then only 10 years old. This is what He said, "Esther, Sheila and Ezekiel (my nephew, who was visiting with us) should wash the carpet and organize the seating room." They were expected to clean the carpet like it had never been cleaned before.

The next duty was allocated to a certain girl who was in transit to my sister's house as household help. She was told to clean the whole house, starting with the toilets.

The next duty was allocated to Lucy. Lucy Silas is a relative who was living with us. Her duty was to prepare breakfast, after which she would wash the cars, mine and my husband's.

The next duty was allocated to Priscilla. She was told that by 5:00 a.m. she should be in the reading room answering some questions she had not finished with that would be used during the meeting.

Mine was the last duty to be allocated. I was expected to go through the materials that I was to share with the group. What I was to go through was so extensive that even by the end of the time allotted I had not finished.

Elizabeth Saidimu

As instructed by the Lord, we all woke up at 5:00, and everybody was soon down to work. No questions were asked because we had been with the Lord for some time, we had learned some of His ways and how He wanted things done. No person can claim to know the Lord fully, but He allows us to have an idea of who He is.

At around 6:30, Jesus called me on my cell phone and told me to go and take a shower. I came to know that each one of us had been called and told the time to bathe. (I know some of the things I write here seem rather unbelievable, but believe me, they are true and is exactly what happened. I would urge you to seek God and confirm with Him the things that I am writing in this book that He asked me to write.)

Jesus Christ said that we could take a break in between to prepare lunch. By 8:00, the family that had promised to come at that time arrived, and we were all ready to get started. The day prior to the meeting, the Lord had told me that the material that we were to go through was a lot and that most people would get tired. He said that some would even fall asleep during the meeting and that among the people who would be completely awake and ready to continue until we finished was one particular member. And He said that I should ask anyone getting tired or sleepy to leave and go home. He also said that I should tell the people that "The freedom to choose is better than slavery." He had said previously that to follow Him

My Visits to Heaven and Hell

and do His will was a choice and that going to Heaven was not a must. Each one had to make a choice; no one would be forced.

Sure enough, when Sunday came and the meeting started, just as the Lord had said, people began to fall asleep. At one point, we had to stop and ask all those who were falling asleep to stand up so that they could wake up. Still, no sooner had they sat back down than they went back to sleep.

Eventually, I was not able to continue because more than half of the members were already asleep. Anyway, it had come to the end of the day, so we agreed to end there. One member didn't agree. She was the one the Lord had said would be strong, and she was opposed to this arrangement. She kept saying that we should finish all the material that Jesus had asked us to go through.

In the process of all of this, I failed to tell the people what the Lord had said about going home. I had been supposed to ask whoever was getting tired to leave, to go on home because going to Heaven was a choice.

The previous day, Priscilla's sister had tried calling her on her cell phone, without success. On this Sunday, she flashed/ signaled and expected Priscilla to call her back. Another issue that surprised me was that Priscilla's cell phone had airtime/credit/units but could not call out. She had to use my mobile when she needed to call anyone.

That night the Lord rebuked us, telling us that if we had not been able to control three families and tell them to leave if they wanted to sleep, how would we be able to control the whole world when He brought them to us? It was the last time the Lord allowed us to meet with the original families. The devil had taken advantage of our disobedience and lack of commitment. God will not work with people who are not committed. The beauty is that one can always go back, ask for forgiveness, change their ways and God will forgive them and still work with them.

This was a very hard day. Jesus took Priscilla's cell phone, which had refused to call out the whole day, and used it to call one of the families and speak to three of their members. This call created a lot of tension and almost split the group. We asked to be forgiven for our failure, and the Lord said that we should pray for four days, as we sought His forgiveness.

After the four days, He forgave us and continued training us, this time, only my family. I thank Jesus Christ very much because of this. To me, it was a very memorable day among many other memorable days that were to follow. Based on this event, I had to make a decision about what to do next. Jesus was very real to me from that day, even though some members started saying that they were not comfortable with the way we claimed He was operating in our family life. This did not change what He wanted to do with me and my family. Instead, the training was even deeper now. He talked to me and referred me to the day that I was commissioned. He reminded me that I would be rejected, abused, and even called a devil worshiper, but that I should always remember that it was about Him, and the battle was His.

Even keeping all of this in mind, I still suffered a lot. I wanted to be accepted by my friends, and I wanted them to believe that what I was saying was true. I cried and asked Jesus what was to happen. He told me to look at a Swahili song he had taught us that says: *"Ulimwenguni mtadhihakiwa na kutukanwa no kukataliwa lakini jipeni moyo kwani mmeshashinda."* (In the world you will be misused, abused and rejected, but be of good cheer for you are already victors). The Lord comforted me throughout this very difficult time. He told me that I should not be bothered by any member saying negative things or even leaving the group. He said that He would bless the people who would believe what He had to say through me. He promised blessings to any person who would follow His teachings given through me. This promise keeps me going to this very day.

When Priscilla woke up, she started asking what had happened to the credit/air time/units that she had on her cell phone. We told her that Jesus had used her mobile phone to call some members. In the days that followed, I had very hard time because some of the members of the Bible study started doubting if indeed I was dealing and talking to Jesus. They convinced one another not to continue with the study. They told me that they needed time to pray and seek guidance from the Lord. One member informed me of this development, that they were seeking the Lord for more guidance.

I told Jesus the same night what the members had said. Another member had indicated that if it was really true that Jesus had been talking to me that I should ask Him to talk to them and not through another person. When I told Jesus about all this, He told me that He is the one who answers prayers. He said, "Suppose they prayed, and their prayers were not answered." I pleaded with the Lord to answer their prayers because the situation was becoming grave. Jesus told me that the battle was His, and from that time on, I had peace of mind.

We continued as a family without the other members. The Lord gave us messages every Sunday. I thank God for I now know that all I need is Jesus Christ and not men. He is the One who draws men to any person, and He has done it for me.

Jesus continued visiting with us as a family every night from 10:30 to 3:30 or 4:00 a.m., depending on the subject He was training us on. My children became aware of His presence, and they would be in "class" on time.

Allow me to mention about the commissioning. One night, Jesus called both Lucy and me and asked if we were ready to serve Him and if we were prepared to be abused, rejected, and misunderstood. We both answered in the affirmative. And these were the vows that we took.

As we were doing this, each in turn, we did not know what was ahead for us. We have been through very hard times because of this commissioning, but I thank God that every day I have grown stronger and learned to love Him more. He said that I would be like Paul and Lucy like Silas. He also said that He was sending us to Macedonia. When I asked Him what He meant by Macedonia, He said that Macedonia was anywhere in the world that He would send us. Later, while in Heaven with Him and Priscilla, He put a big golden hat on me, like those we see bishops wearing. He put a smaller hat of gold on Priscilla. He told me that this was for service. In this way, the Lord ordained me for service.

Chapter One

Some of the Lessons the Lord Taught Us

Brethren, allow Jesus to operate in your life. He is interested in you, and He wants to sort you out. If you allow Him to operate in you and to make sure that you diminish, so that He may increase in you, I can assure you that your life will never be the same again.

I would like to share with you a testimony among the many that I love sharing. It's about how God healed me from uterine cancer. The doctors had asked me to inform my employer of my condition and request to be given light duties. I was the custodian of the keys to the bank strong room or vault (where cash and important documents are stored). Bankers especially can appreciate the importance placed on the holders of such keys. If the key holder does not report for duty, there could be no business that day.

When I informed my boss (who was very helpful and considerate) about my diagnosis, the first thing she did was to withdraw the keys for the strong room

My Visits to Heaven and Hell

from me. After the keys were withdrawn, my juniors mostly stopped bothering me with work. One would be coming to my office to bring me some work and just go back before I could say anything. To me, this was the beginning of death. Remember that I was just a young believer. My husband and I would go to the clinic every Tuesday for counseling and an update on my condition.

The devil had been preaching to me that the cancer problem had come about because of my salvation. He made sure that he repeated it often, suggesting that I reconsider my decision to serve the Lord. These were very trying moments, and I know some of you who are reading this could be going through the preachings of the devil. Remind him that he is a liar and he was reduced to zero by Jesus Christ. He should keep his lies to himself and his demons.

I went to the laboratory every fortnight (two weeks), and the test results were what the doctor would use to update us. Then one day Jesus sent me some help in a very mysterious way. A lady from our head office came one morning, and as she greeted me, she asked me how things were. As I was talking to her, I could hear two different voices. One of them was loud and was telling me not to tell about my condition, and the other was faint and it was telling me that I should tell her. I finally told her that I had cancer.

She did not seem surprised like the rest of the people that I would share with. She said to me, "Since you are born-again why don't you just pray?"

The way she said it made it look so easy. She went on to say, "After everyone in your house has gone to sleep, go into a room where you can be alone and open your hands before the Lord and tell Him this, 'Jesus, remove this demon called cancer from me.' "

I did it that very night, and I saw myself holding a large black substance the size of a rugby ball. It was oval in shape. The substance started bleeding until my hands had nothing more to hold.

The blood eventually was spread and flew out, and to this day I am healed of cancer. That was more than thirteen years ago, and the Lord has continued to be real in my life. He confirmed to me that He is the One who healed me and that He wants to use me for His Kingdom. He wanted me to share with you this testimony so that you may be encouraged and know that He is able. It does not matter what the problem is. God is more powerful than any problem on this earth. He has healed many people, some of whom the evil one has stopped from testifying of the goodness of our Lord. Far too many people have given the glory that belongs to God alone to others, and that is so wrong.

This is just one of the many testimonies the Lord has continued to give me, to constantly remind me that He is Lord. From that time, I have seen God in many ways, and I have prayed for sick people who have also been healed.

But allow me to discuss some of the lessons we learned from the Lord.

CHAPTER TWO

Enter Priscilla

I would like to introduce Priscilla. I had always gotten house help through my mother-in-law. She would get girls from our home area, Loitokitok. Since we were at the border of Kenya and Tanzania, some of the girls would be from Tanzania. This time she brought me a girl I thought was too young for the job, but when I talked to her I discovered that she was already an adult. That made me comfortable to have her in my house. Her name was Priscilla.

Before Priscilla came, a relative named Lucy had lived with us and helped us around the house, but she was due for college and wanted to train as a nurse. She had been in my house already for about nine months, so she was able to train Priscilla in all the areas of housework. In the process, the Spirit of the Lord spoke to me, and I requested Lucy, who had been born-again for more than six years, to start spending time with Priscilla during the day, reading the Bible and praying.

I reasoned with them that since they were two of them in the house and there wasn't enough work to keep them both busy the whole day, they should spend about two hours daily reading the Bible and praying. I gave them Bibles, and they started. I would find out from Lucy how the training was going. I made sure that they spent time in the Word because Lucy was to leave for college in two month's time, and I was trusting God that Priscilla would have gained something from Lucy before she left. Until then, Priscilla had not been born-again.

One day, after a month of this, Lucy asked me if I could spare some time to pray with Priscilla, for Priscilla wanted to give her life to Jesus Christ. That made me very happy. We prayed, and Priscilla gave her life to Jesus. After her salvation, things went along well … until one day I came home and found her asleep. I asked Lucy why Priscilla was sleeping during the day, and I was informed that she had been having headaches.

I called Priscilla and, at the same time, sent Lucy to the shops to buy some items that we needed for supper. It was about 6:30 in the evening. When Priscilla came, I asked her what the problem was. I tried to enquire from her if she had been having that problem before coming to my house, but she said no. Before we had talked for very long, she suddenly fainted and fell down.

When Priscilla came to me, I tried talking to her again, to find out if she'd had that problem before, but she said no. I called my Pastor (Pastor Jeremiah) and asked him what could have been the problem. He told me that the next time it happened I should speak to the spirit that was causing Priscilla to fall. Little did I know that this was to be the beginning of many great experiences. From that day to this, my life has never been the same again.

One month after Priscilla's salvation, a relative of mine called and asked me to loan her my house help for a few days, as she looked for some new help for herself. Her employee had left her suddenly. She knew that Lucy was still in the house and that there wasn't a lot of work to be done there. I felt comfortable with this and told her to come by and get Priscilla. This relative came for Priscilla on a Monday, and until then Priscilla had been okay. I had no idea what was about to follow.

A day after Priscilla had been picked up by my relative, I was in the process of talking with my pastor, and I mentioned to him that I had sent Priscilla to stay with that relative. He said that it was probably not good that I had lent her out. She was my child now, and I had to take good care of her. At the time, I did not understand what he meant by her being "my child." I would understand it later.

Four days after Priscilla had left, my relative called to say that the girl was very sick. She was wondering whether to take her to a hospital or what she should do. The Spirit of the Lord quickly reminded me that I needed to see Priscilla before she was taken to hospital, so I told my relative that I would come to see them the following day.

Chapter Three

Powers of Darkness

This was the day when I experienced the powers of darkness for the first time in my life. I had been seeing demonized people on TV, televangelists casting out demons, but I had never seen it face to face. When I got to the house, the owners had to go to work, and that meant that I was left alone with Priscilla, Lucy, my two children and my relative's children. I confronted Priscilla and asked her what she was suffering from. What she explained did not make sense. She said that she was feeling sick and that she had pain in her entire body. Then she started crying.

I asked Priscilla to kneel down, so that we could pray together. This had become the order in our house. When anyone was sick, before we thought of any other remedy, we first prayed. She knew this, since she had been in our house for more than two months now. This became one of our greatest experiences in how God can work through His children. Instead of kneeling, Priscilla fell down and started wriggling like a snake on the living room floor. She became so strong and so violent that Lucy and I could not hold her. Each time we tried to restrain her, she flung us aside.

At that point I remembered what Pastor Jeremiah had said to me, that I should ask who she was. I asked her who she was, and for some time she did not reply. Then, after a while, demons started to speak to me through her. They told me that they had been sent from the ocean and that their work was to kill and drink blood. They said that they had left her about a month before (this was when she had given her life to Jesus Christ), but I had allowed them to come back by moving her out from my protective cover. They said that they had entered into her the moment she entered my relative's house and that I had no authority over them, since they were not in my house. But, according to John 8:44, the devil is a liar and the father of lies. As you continue reading, you will realize that he was lying about her not being in my house.

I commanded the demons to leave. In reply, they asked me to call a pastor if I really wanted them to go. I could not think of any pastor who could come at quick notice, so I would have to gather courage and fight back.

I told the demons that I was the pastor for the day. They again told me that they would not go since their master had told them not to go back, that the place where they had come from was full. We talked back and forth and fought for about two and a half hours, and I became very tired.

Elizabeth Saidimu

The demons told me that they had killed one of Priscilla's sisters and that they were in the process of killing the second one. They said that they had no intention of killing Priscilla; they wanted to use her for their work.

They told me that Priscilla's mother was prayerful but they had been able to take control of her father, who is the head of the family. As we continued talking, the demons would sometimes refuse to answer my questions, but I told them I would call fire in the name of Jesus Christ. They pleaded with me and begged me not to call down fire or to use the name of "that person." They would not call Jesus Christ by name. They gave me a lot of stories (which I may not put in writing). Keep in mind that at this time I had no training on casting out demons. I was just saying what I had seen and heard pastors say on TV while they cast out demons. I kept on calling down fire in the name of the Lord Jesus Christ. At one point the demons told me that they were very tired and asked to be given a few minutes' break.

Finally, the demons told me that they would go out because I had burned them so much, but they vowed to come back as long as Priscilla was not under my protection. They told me that they wanted to use Priscilla to cause accidents so that they could get blood to drink. I asked them if they wanted my blood, as I was willing to give them one cup. They said they were not interested in my blood. (If you are born-again, demons cannot accept your blood).

My Visits to Heaven and Hell

This was such an experience for me and, as usual, God was faithful. He gave me strength to fight demons for the first time, with no prior experience of such things. I did not even know what to say to them, but He gave me utterance. It was a very long day for me, but God was with me all through it all. Little did I know that I was to go through this for the next three years, in fact for many more years to come.

On this particular day, the demons left after that long fight. I did not think they would come back. But as soon as I was out of my relative's house, they came back. They told me that when I had ordered them to leave, they stayed outside the door and waited for me to leave. Then, once I was gone, they came back, this time with more force.

Now the demons wanted to kill Priscilla because she had refused to do what they had wanted. She told me that a man came into her bedroom as she was sleeping and ordered her to go to the top of a building and cast her herself off, to kill herself. She refused. He then went to the kitchen and came back with a kitchen knife and wanted to kill her with it, but she called on the name of Jesus Christ, and the knife dropped from his hand.

The man was now willing to cooperate with Priscilla. He told her to go to the road. There he would turn her into a piece of paper, and any vehicle that would run over that paper would roll over and the people inside it would die. That way, blood would be available for the demons. These are some of the methods they use. When we see a lot of accidents taking place, we can know that demons are at work.

Priscilla refused to honor this request, as well, and because of this, she became very sick. This all took place after I had left, and in three days time she was very sick. I had no control over what was happening. In fact, I did not yet even have an explanation of what was happening.

After all of this happened, my relative wanted to bring Priscilla back to my house because she was just adding to the problems that were already there. Instead, the Lord had me offer to go and pick her up. Later I learned that the devil had planned to kill them both as they drove to our house.

After those two incidents, I was in a lot of trouble with my relatives, especially my mother, who told me that I had sent my relative a bad helper to stay with her children. I did not really know how to defend myself from all that was being said, because I was in a situation that I could not explain. I was very happy with all the experiences I was having, but I was getting myself in such trouble with relatives and friends who could not understand what was happening. I couldn't blame them. Even I did not understand what was happening, but I had peace within.

Three days later I went back to my relative's house to pick up Priscilla. When I got there, she looked very unhappy. I asked her what was the problem, and she said that she was feeling very sick, a sickness that could not be explained. We decided to pray. When we started praying, she fell down and started moving like a snake again. I asked who it was, and the answer came: "I am Lucifer." This day the fight was more intense. The demons would not listen. They were so strong that I got tired.

I continued to rebuke Satan in the name of Jesus Christ. The demons were really burning, but since I did not know that I should bind them first, so that they would not keep moving in and out of her, I simply kept on rebuking them and calling for fire to fall on them. The demons, now more than ten, kept on changing, so that the one who was burning could go out, and another one could come in. In this way I learned that one cannot achieve much if demons are free to move in and out of a person because they call for reinforcement from other demons.

Once you bind them, they continue burning until they ask to be allowed to leave. At this point, you should instruct them where to go and that they are never to come back. Due to my lack of knowledge, it took me many hours to ensure that the demons burned and decide to go. Later in my training, the Lord gave me information on how to deliver someone. This is what He said should be done:

Elizabeth Saidimu

Conducting a Deliverance Session:

i. Keep crowds away. Do not cast out demons when a crowd is present (especially if they are non-Christians.) Jesus Christ quickly rebuked the evil spirit and cast it out when He saw an inquisitive crowd approaching (see Mark 9:25).

ii. There are cases known where an unclean spirit has left one person and entered into inquisitive unbelieving onlookers. Some church leaders prepare a room with carpet or quilts on the floor and pillows around the wall. This padding prevents the demonized person from physically injuring themselves. Often the demonized writhe and flail about when the demons depart.

iii. When involved in deliverance, it is good to start with praising and then worshiping God in the Spirit. Praising God builds your faith.

iv. Worship brings the manifest presence (the anointing) of the Holy Spirit into the situation. Sing worshipful choruses and songs, to prepare the room for God to come. Anointed musicians playing their instruments and singers worshipfully adoring Jesus Christ can create the atmosphere where His will is more readily implemented.

v. Have the demonized person kneel and acknowledge (say with his mouth): "My deliverance comes only through Jesus Christ and His victory over the devil and his angles. I believe Jesus Christ is Lord! I bow my knee, and I confess this with my mouth, and I declare: *"That at the name of Jesus every knee shall bow, of things in heaven [the angles and saints], and things in earth, and things under the earth [the demons]"* (Philippians 2:10). "I know the truth, and the truth sets me free, so if the Son shall make me free, I'll be free indeed" (see John 8:32 and 36).

vi. Use the name of Jesus Christ to enforce the victory He gained over Satan and his forces, *"Wherefore God also hath highly exalted him, and given him a name which is above every name"* (Philippians 2:9). Mark 16:17 says, *"In my name shall they cast out devils."*

vii. Remember, this is all as a result of the shedding of the blood of Jesus Christ on the cross.

That day we took more than two hours for the demons to leave. They asked me if they could go into a river, which is near my relative's house. I said no. I told them that all rivers belong to Jesus Christ and that they had no right to go into any river.

After they left, the next voice I heard was a thanksgiving prayer and praise, the kind of prayer that was made was one that I had never heard before. It was so well coordinated. I later learned that the prayer was being made by someone who was standing in the living room. He was dressed in a white robe, and only Priscilla could see him. The rest of us could not.

After the prayer, I asked Priscilla where she had been. She told me that the devil had taken her to a very large supermarket which had everything in it. It was bigger than any we had ever taken her to in Kenya. It had all sorts of things for sale, even cars. The devil told her that if she was going to listen to him and agree to work for him, he would give her that supermarket and everything in it. Still she refused.

Next he again took her up on a tall building and wanted to throw her down from there and kill her. It was at this point that Jesus Christ came and picked her up. He brought her back to the living room, where we were praying. She told me that He had been the One who was praying the prayer I mentioned above. She said that even as we talked He was still standing there. She could see Him, and she also thought that we were seeing Him too. When she knew that we were not, she wondered why we could not see Him, since He was standing right in front of us.

After the prayer was over, the voice asked me to pray for my relative's family, including the children, for protection. I was also told that when I got to my house, I should pray for my own family members. This prayer was to cover my entire family – my husband and children.

The devil is a liar and the father of all lies. The demons had told me that I should not order them around, since they had not come to my house. And they had made it very clear that they would not come to my house. This was a lie that I had bought, and because of it, I thought that if I took Priscilla home to our house the demons would no longer torment her. This day, as I took her with me, I did not expect to be fighting any more demons, but this was just to be the beginning. Casting out demons from Priscilla would go on for the next three years.

During those three years, I visited Hell and Heaven, and I still do. In fact, I frequent heaven. Heaven is home. It's our Father's home, and we are free to visit there as often as we wish. If you want to visit your earthly father, you don't need your brother or sister to go along, do you? The same applies to a visit to Heaven. You only need Jesus Christ.

A month before all of this, my pastor had sent me a text message which read:

> "I believe you had a blessed day. Arise, pray, and watch. Jesus Christ is doing new things. Just trust in Him for His Holy Spirit and wait upon Him. Stay tuned and very alert."

Elizabeth Saidimu

After sending this text massage, he called me and asked me to make sure that I wrote it down, for it had a lot of meaning. He told me that Jesus said that He had come to my house. Of course, this did not make sense to me at the moment. I kept him informed of what was happening, and he encouraged me to keep praying and to remember the text message that he had sent.

I sometimes wondered: if Jesus Christ had really come into my house, then I expected some good things to be happening there, and I did not expect to be fighting with demons. All he said was that I was on the right track and that I should call upon the Lord and thank Him for what was happening.

One day the Lord asked me to write this book. He told me that the main characters should be Priscilla and myself. She is the fifth-born of a family of six. She was called by God at the tender age of ten. What I am writing about her did not come from her, but from Jesus Christ Himself. He told me that when Priscilla was ten years old, one Sunday she had gone to church. Her mother was traveling, so Priscilla did not have anything for the offering. When she saw other children giving their offering, she was so very sad that she started crying. When she got home, she started praying. She was asking God to help her. In the process of this prayer, Jesus Christ came to her, but His appearance was as a man. He asked her if she was ready to follow Him, so that He could help

My Visits to Heaven and Hell

her solve her problems. He told me that out of fear she had said yes. It was at this time that the Lord came into her life and started leading her.

The Lord directed Priscilla to a certain Catholic nun in the church she used to attend. The Lord used this nun to teach her the ways of God. Within a short time, Priscilla started teaching other children the ways of the Lord. She would pass by the church for prayers before going to school. Because of this, the other children would tease her and say that she was pretending to be nice, but Jesus Christ was always with her.

Priscilla managed to finish her primary school education, and then she was to join a secondary school. Initially she was to go to a boarding school, but she refused and, instead, asked to be taken to a day school (where one goes to school and comes home in the evening). She joined the day school and was happy to be in school.

Jesus Christ told me one time, as she was going home from school, she came upon some boys intent on raping a certain girl. They even had a knife. He told me that as small as Priscilla was, He gave her enough strength that she was able to rescue the girl. She beat up the boys and took their knife home with her. The next day, one of the boys came to apologize and ask for the knife.

Jesus Christ told me that He had prepared her for eleven years to come to my house. He had been with her all through those years, but then peer pressure started to interfere with her good intentions, and she had started to become just like any other child her age.

Jesus Christ was preparing her for something bigger and very different from what she was settling for. Her friends were distracting her from what the Lord was calling her for, just like Samson of the Bible (see Judges chapters 13 and 14). Jesus Christ told me that He made her father to stop paying school fees for her, because she had gotten herself in bad company, and it was going to destroy her calling. Her father actually stopped paying the school fees, and in addition to this, he chased her away from home. The only choice that Jesus Christ left for her was to go to her aunt's home, and that aunt just happened to be my relative by marriage.

Around that same time, Jesus Christ created a need by allowing my house help to go away, and it was at that time that I asked my mother-in-law to find me some suitable girl. This is one of the reasons that we are told in the Scriptures to give thanks at all times. I might have complained that I would be without help in the house, not knowing that the Lord had prepared a special person for me. Indeed, all things work together for good (see Roman 8:28).

While Priscilla was at her aunt's place, Jesus Christ told me that He visited her many times. One of these times that He visited her, He found her praying. He came to her in the form of a very bright light, and she became very frightened, stopped praying, and went

My Visits to Heaven and Hell

to sleep. The following day she told her aunt about this experience. The aunt could not understand it. She sent for a certain catholic priest in their local church, and he told them that they should continue praying. Because no one understood the experience, they equated it with a bad dream.

When Priscilla came to our house, she told me that she was not born-again, and I asked Lucy to spend at least two or three hours each day with her in prayer and reading the Word of God. This was how Priscilla got saved. It was after this that she went to my relative's house when demons started manifesting themselves through her.

After I got her out of my relative's house, the demons did not stop. They now followed her into my house, and I would fight them every day. By this time, I was getting to know many things. These devils would try to persuade me to join their camp.

The devil will follow you because of the calling you have. He intends to kill the calling in your life, and that's why we should be careful and ground ourselves in the knowledge of our God.

The fighting went on for about three years. A month after she had come back to our house from my relative's house, as I was casting out demons that had attacked her, a voice came and said, "I am Jesus Christ." At that moment, the whole house went silent. You could have heard a pin drop. It was after this that our Bible class with Jesus Christ started. Just as I had mentioned earlier, our classes would begin at 10:00 p.m. and go on, sometimes until 5:00 in the morning. On some days, I would just have time to take a shower and go to work. Still, no one at work would know that I had not slept the night before. Brethren, rest comes from God. If He says that you shouldn't sleep, you can operate normally, and you will not get tired. It is God who holds the world. He is the One who orders the sun and the moon in their place.

Let me narrate some of the experiences that I had with Jesus Christ and, of course, Satan. Remember, the more you seek God, the more the devil is interested in you. Some of the experiences cannot be put on paper, but I know that what I will put down will help readers to seek the Lord Jesus Christ even more and to know that our God is real. All the things that He has said in the Bible are true and will come to pass. We should know and trust God, for He has such love for us. He said, *"I am come that they might have life, and that they might have it more abundantly"* (John 10:10).

Chapter Four

More Fighting with Satan and His Demons

Every day, when I arrived home from work, I would find Priscilla indifferent. If I asked her how her day was; she would simply say that it had been bad. This forced me to want to find out why she would say that her day had been bad. As she narrated to me what might have happened that day, she would be taken away, and in her place there would be demons. These are the demons that I would have to fight with to release her. Many times, it would take more than two hours to get them to go.

During these fights, they would tear her clothes and even mine, pluck off her hair or disturb any other person or thing in the room where we would be doing the warfare. Often we were both left with wounds on our hands. Sometime the fight would become so bad that I would be forced to call on Lucy to assist me, and she, too, would also be left with wounds.

My Visits to Heaven and Hell

I will never forget the day when Priscilla wanted to jump over the gate because the demons had instructed her to commit suicide by throwing herself into the road. A relative who had come to visit us was strong and worked with the Kenyan Army. When he heard the commotion, he ran out to see what he could do. I was still in my bedroom when all of this was happening. He tried to pull her away from the gate, but she turned on him and was beating him up. The fight stopped only when I got out there and called on the name of Jesus.

The devil does not fear status. He only fears the name of Jesus Christ, and it is not just anyone who can call on that name and get a response. It is important to know that Jesus Christ knows you and that you have a right as His child. Jesus declared, *"In my name shall they cast out devils; they shall speak with new tongues"* (Mark 16:17). One needs to have a personal relationship with Jesus Christ to be able to fight Satan. Otherwise, he can turn on you. You need to know that you have the authority over him. Remember the seven sons of Sceva. Their story if found in Acts 19:14-16.

Many times the demons would throw Priscilla on the ground so hard that we thought that her head would surely crack. At other times, she would be forced to bang against the wall over and over again. When I attempted to stop her, I would be thrown against the wall or onto the bed. The demons would be so strong that only the name of Jesus Christ could calm them down. I could sometimes call the name of Jesus Christ for more than two hours, and still the demons would not listen. When I enquired of the Lord, He told me that I was undergoing training, and He was the One who had allowed the fighting to take place.

One time the Lord asked me if I wanted the fighting to stop, but His Spirit reminded me of what He had told me, that it was all training. It was for Him to know when the fighting should stop. At this time, I was quick to say no. *"And he said unto me, Son of man, can these bones live? And I answered, O LORD God, thou knowest"* (Ezekiel 37:3).

At other times, Priscilla would go under the bed and start banging her head against the floor. It was very difficult to stop her because I would not be able to get under the very low bed. Demons would even cause her to go under seats that had very small spaces, where none of us could reach her. We would be forced to keep pulling out furniture the whole night.

At other times, the demons would cause Priscilla to scream very loudly. This usually occurred at night, around 1:30 a.m., when everybody else was asleep. If I tried controlling them, they would cause her to run out of the house and say that they would use her to kill someone through an accident on the road. It took some time before I knew how to bind these demons and to get them to stay in one place. Until then, I needed to keep all the keys to the house with me and make sure that before we started all the doors were securely locked.

My Visits to Heaven and Hell

Even though I kept the keys, so that the demons could not make her go out of the house, it didn't work. I was in training, and the Lord wanted me to experience all of this.

It was worse if the demons managed to get Priscilla into the bathroom. They would then lock the door and cause her to hit her head really hard against the bathroom wall. Sometimes they would pluck out her hair so that I was unable to control what was happening. Whenever she was locked up in anyplace where we had no access, it would take me a long time to get her free. This went on for a while, until I came to learn that by the name of Jesus I could stop what was happening in the bathroom, without being inside it.

At other times, Priscilla's notebooks and clothes would go missing, and the demons would own up the fact that they have taken them. At one point, the Lord asked me to buy her a Bible. She used it for few months, and then it went missing. The demons told me that they had taken it because when she read it, she would know many things, which might make it difficult for them to win her over.

Demons would cause Priscilla to hide in the house, even if all the doors were locked, and it would always take me a long time to find her. I couldn't think of going to sleep as long as the demons were still there, because they would make sure we didn't sleep. So if she went missing, I would have to search the whole house. This was very difficult because while I was busy looking for her in one room, she moved to another room. It was a four-bedroom house, and that made it complicated to track her. She could even run into the kitchen, after I had already looked there.

One night I could not find Priscilla, so I decided to go on to sleep, since it was really getting very late. Just as I had gotten into bed, the demons started beating her up. She cried so much that I had to come to her rescue. Then, by the time I got out of my room, there was no noise, and I could not trace her again. This happened many nights. Remember that all of this was allowed by the Lord for the purpose of this book and for more training for me.

One night, as Priscilla and I were praying, demons came and entered her. She ran into the kitchen and came back with a kitchen knife, ready to stab me. We struggled until the knife dropped. As I said before, many of the details of the fights we had cannot be put into print, and this went on for three long years.

Sometimes it became very difficult to keep any liquid detergents in the house, because the demons would cause Priscilla to drink everything. This included any sort of medicine, any detergents, and even Kerosene. You name it, and she drank it. We had to ensure that anything she might possibly drink was locked away, so I kept most of it in my room and allowed it to be used only when I was home.

Priscilla was never allowed to enter my personal bedroom. At the time, I was still in full-time employ-

My Visits to Heaven and Hell

ment, working from 8:00 a.m. to 5:00 p.m., and I was an evening student from 5:30 to 8:30 each night. Training with Jesus would start at about 10:00 and continue to as late as 5:00 in the morning on some days.

These demons tried hard to get me to renounce Jesus Christ and join their camp, and in doing so, they would tell me stories about the many people whom their master assisted in business or even with favors, with authority, with promotions in their work places, etc. Demons are very good at marketing their "product," as you know, and marketers can confirm this.

If you are selling a product, it's usually beneficial to give the names of some of the people using your product so that would-be buyers can verify with them. In the same manner, demons would give me some of the names of the people whom Satan was assisting or those who had benefited from his favors. These included people that I knew. For sure, these things happen. People get favors. Businesses blossom, and promotions come easily. The difference is that what the devil gives does not last, and it is usually very expensive. *"While we look not at the things which are seen, but at the things which are not seen: for the things which are seen are temporal; but the things which are not seen are eternal"* (2 Corinthians 4:18). Some of the people whom the devil had told me he had cause to be promoted, as of the writing of this book, have lost their jobs. Others who were doing so well in business due to the "help" from Satan are now out of business.

When one allows Satan to use them, it might appear as if they are doing well, but deep down they are very unhappy people. Most of them have sacrificed their children, spouses, parents, and other relatives so that they may be promoted or have given lots of money. When I see what the devil does to people who do not know his ways, I am so moved that I want to preach to them there and then and help them to know that they do not have to continue suffering, that Jesus died for them, and they can be free – if they choose Jesus.

Dear reader, as you are reading this book, please know that the devil has no secrets. Anything that he gives to those who are serving him, he will brag about it to others. He will use such people and their names to get others to come to him. He will give you examples and names of the people that he is helping, so that you are pulled toward accepting him. He would often discuss with me the people on his payroll. I am talking about real people, people whom I know, who are doing very well in life.

Please, don't be bothered with people's achievements. You never know how they do it. Just trust in the Lord Jesus Christ, and He will work in your life and make it what He created you for. Anything that comes from Satan is not permanent; it is very expensive and will destroy you and your family. Believe me when I say this: I have seen it happen, and that is why the Lord wants me to have this information out to every person that is looking for freedom.

My Visits to Heaven and Hell

When the devil is marketing to you, he will never tell you the other side of the story. He will never tell you what is expected of you. In my case, the devil offered to be giving me Kshs. 50,000 per day. This would have been about US $850 every day. This was a lot of money then. My salary for a whole month was less. I asked the devil what I would pay in return. He said that I would have to go and be with him after ten years. This meant death. If I had accepted Satan's offer, I would have died ten years later. Many people would have been envious of me, not knowing that I had sold my soul for the "good life."

It is not easy to make people understand the ways of Satan because, in most cases, the children of God appear to be having more problems than those of the devil. Nevertheless, be encouraged. These things don't last. Just look back later, and you will see what has happened to those people who have frustrated the children of God. *"For he that toucheth you toucheth the apple of his eye"* (Zechariah 2:8). It may not be seen immediately, but eventually it will all become clear. Satan's rewards are short-term, but what God gives is good and permanent.

The beauty about the fights that I used to have with Satan and his demons was that after the demons went, even if it was at 2:00 a.m., the Lord Jesus Christ would come and go through with me what I had learned. He would then start His teachings, which would take more hours. Sometimes this study would be with the children, but at other times, He would allow the children to go to bed, and I would be left alone with Him.

I received a lot of training from Jesus Christ Himself. He told me that the Bible was the cover of a book that had not yet been written. He said that if the Bible had been fully written out and all the details of the insights narrated in it would have been included, there would have been no space large enough to store it on the earth. That is why we require the Holy Spirit to enable us to understand the Bible. That's why Paul, in 1 Corinthians 2:14, says that *"But the natural man receiveth not the things of the Spirit of God: for they are foolishness unto him: neither can he know them, because they are spiritually discerned."* The Lord would explain to me why one preacher can preach from the some scripture verse and have a different explanation from another, yet they both have their message from the Lord, and it is a message that will be a blessing to His people. He gave me details of issues I cannot talk about just yet, until He allows me to do so in the future.

I learned a lot from the Lord. Some of the things that I learned from Him I had never heard anyone talk about. Some of the things I learned I can only share with individuals who can take them in. Jesus is the best teacher that we will ever know.

Before He stopped me from talking about the things that I had learned from Him, I got myself in trouble with my friends. I would share with them what the Lord had taught me, not knowing that some information would be used against me by some of them. I had some very difficult times. The problem that I was having was from BELIEVERS and still is!

Take note. I was very excited, and I would share what I had learned from Him with friends and relatives. Within a very short time, some of them started isolating me and saying that I had a strange spirit. It was then that the Lord cautioned me that I should not talk about my experience with Him or the devil with others until He allowed me to do so. He told me to write this book so that many people can learn and know the operations of Satan and know that God is God and that He has power above all other powers.

Chapter Five

My First Trip to Hell

Before I tell you about my first trip to Hell, allow me to insert some biblical material related to underworld or netherworld that will help readers understand it:

A SCRIPTURAL DESCRIPTION OF THE UNDER/NETHERWORLD

1) **Tartarus** (1 Peter 3:19, 2 Peter 2:4 and Jude 1:6-7)
   This prison is a special one for fallen angels who sinned before the flood. No human beings or demons ever go to this prison. See note, 2 Peter 2:4.

2) **Paradise** (Luke 16:19-31 and 23:43)
   This was the abode of the righteous after physical death, where they were held captive by the devil against their will, until Christ conquered death, Hell, and the grave. It is now empty of the righteous, who go to Heaven at death, since Christ captured the captives in Hell and took

them to Heaven with Him when He ascended on high. (See Luke 16:22, Ephesians 4:8-10 and Hebrews 2:14-15).

3) **The Abyss or Bottomless Pit**
(Luke 8:26-31, Romans 10:7, Revelation 9:1-3, 11, 11:7, 17:8, and 20:1-10).
This is the abode of demons and some angelic beings. No human soul or spirit ever goes to the Abyss. The O.T. Hebraic equivalent is Abaddon and is translated *destruction* (see Job 26:6, 28:22, 31:12, Psalm 88:11, Proverbs 15:11 and 27:20).

4) **The Lake of Fire**
This is the eternal Hell and perdition of all: Satan, fallen angels, demons and wicked men (see Revelation 20:6, 11-15, 21:8 and 22:15). It is the same as *gehenna* (see Luke 12:5). It is the final Hell prepared for the devil and his angels (Matthew 25:41) and is eternal in duration (Isaiah 66:22- 24, Matthew 25:46, Revelation 14:9-14, 19:20 and 20:10-15).

5) **Hell** (Matthew 16:18, Luke 16:19-1).
This is the torment compartment of Sheol/ Hades. Hell is not the grave, but a place of consciousness and torment where those who are physically dead go. Their souls and spirits have always gone there and will always go there until

the end of the Millennium. It is not the Lake of Fire, but there is horror and tormenting of the souls and spirits also in this part of Hell. Then the wicked will be brought out of here to be reunited with their resurrected bodies.

OTHER AREAS IN THE NETHERWORLD

Since the netherworld is so expansive, it should be noted that there are parts of Hell where the spirits of the living dead are held captive by Satan against their will. 2 Timothy 2:26: *"And that they may recover themselves out of the snare of the devil, who are taken captive by him at his will."*

Since man is born in sin, those who do not know God are still held captive by Satan in some dimension of Hell. The Scriptures allude to people being held captive, bound, in prison and captivity or bondage (see Isaiah 61:1) and also says that Jesus came to seek and to save the lost (see Luke 19:10) and to set the captives free (see Luke 4:18 and Isaiah 61:1).

Remember, Satan steals people through deception, he kills (separates) them by separating them from God through sin, and lastly, he destroys them completely by killing them physically and spiritually, to never ever know Christ (see John 10:10). However, Jesus has come so that men, instead of dying spiritually, may have eternal life and have it abundantly. It is for such a reason that He was made manifest to destroy the

My Visits to Heaven and Hell

works of Satan (1 John 3:8). God also rescues people from the domain and control of darkness (Satan) and transfers them into the Kingdom of His dear Son in whom there is redemption and forgiveness of sins by His blood. Paul wrote:

> *Giving thanks unto the Father, which hath made us meet to be partakers of the inheritance of the saints in light: who hath delivered us from the power of darkness, and hath translated us into the kingdom of his dear Son: in whom we have redemption through his blood, even the forgiveness of sins).*
>
> Colossians 1:12-14

In this part of the Netherworld:
1. There are prisoners or those held captive by Satan (see Luke 4:18 and 13:11).
2. There are prisons, chambers where they are held (see Proverbs 7:27).
3. This is a place of gross darkness (see Psalm 107:14).
4. There are snares, terrors, anguish, pain, grief, sorrow and much trouble there (see Psalm 116:3).
5. Those who are in bondage are *"ensnared"* there (see Psalm 18:4-6).
6. Some of those in bondage work there (see Job 17:13).
7. The captives held there are in chains or cords (see 2 Samuel 22:6).

8. These captives need to be delivered from the gross darkness (see Psalm 107:14, Isaiah 61:1 and Luke 4:18).
9. They can be delivered (Psalm 30:3 and 86:13)
10. The person who delivers them must break the chains that hold them there (see Psalm 107:14).
11. Jesus delivers men and women from captivity, bondage, deformity, sickness, sin, etc. (see Matthew 8:16).
12. Those who are ensnared there are the living dead (see Psalm 18:4-6).
13. Jesus, as God, can visit Sheol/Hell (see Job 26:6). Psalm 139:8: *"If I ascend up into heaven, thou art there: if I make my bed in hell, behold, thou art there."* Jesus is in Heaven, but He can visit Hell at will.
14. It is dwelling place for the spirits of the living wicked (see Psalm 49:15).
15. It is a place where one can go alive, as part of the living dead (see Psalm 55:15 and Proverbs 1:12).
16. The people there, because they are bound, cannot praise God. The love of God is not in that place (see Psalm 88:11 and Isaiah 61:1).
17. The activities and occupations of people on earth are connected to either Heaven or Sheol (see Proverbs 5:5 and Proverbs 7:27).
18. Satan's deception leads to the gloom and doom of that place (see Proverbs 15:24).

My Visits to Heaven and Hell

19. Sheol is never satisfied (see Proverbs 27:19-21).
20. Sheol is a cruel place (see Song of Solomon 8:6).
21. Sheol has no class. The poor, rich, mighty and weak are all there (see Isaiah 14:9).
22. When Jesus rescues and delivers His people from Sheol, He sets them free indeed and keeps them completely out of Sheol. John 8:36: *"If the Son therefore shall make you free, ye shall be free indeed."* Colossians 1:13: *"Who hath delivered us from the power of darkness, and hath translated us into the kingdom of his dear Son: in whom we have redemption through his blood, even the forgiveness of sins."*

My First Trip

One night I had been fighting with demons, when the Lord appeared and asked me to come with Him. He took me to Hell, to the first basement. I was to visit this area for the next few weeks.

When the Lord took me to Hell, He stood aside and allowed me to see what demons were doing to people there. On this basement level, there were many coffins, dirty white in color. All of them had people inside, some up to three people. It was rare to find a coffin with only one person in it. When people are confined in these coffins, they do not die, but they also cannot breathe. They suffer so much that when you get them out they don't even know where to go.

Elizabeth Saidimu

If demons came and took Priscilla away, I could go and get her back from one of these basements. The times I visited this floor, my main business there was to look for Priscilla and get her out of a coffin. In the name of Jesus Christ, I was able to open between four to ten coffins each night. Since a coffin would be having at least three people, in one night I could rescue about thirty people out of the bondage of Satan. As I opened the coffins one by one, I would eventually find the one Priscilla was in.

After I got the people out of these coffins, the Lord had established a sort of first-aid room in a tent structure. I would take the people there, and Jesus would tie them with a golden ribbon. Once they were tied I would walk with them, using some established stairs. These stairs were just big enough for two people, and they were made of gold. It felt like you were walking on fire, and yet you were not burned. The stairs pass through some very dark places, but with me ahead of the people, holding on to their ribbon, nothing could happen to us.

After walking up the stairs, we would come to a river of blood, and I would lead the people into this river and submerge them in the blood of Jesus Christ. Jesus would be seated at the end of the river. When we got there, I would make the people stand, as if in a parade, and I would pray for them, and He would deliver them. (The cover of this book depicts this reality).

My Visits to Heaven and Hell

After these prayers, I could leave the presence of the Lord, and the people would be free. All of this time, Priscilla would be among them. When I came back to my prayer room, I would find that she was now doing well. The demons had left her. What surprised me most, especially the first time this happened, was that when I asked her where she had been, she narrated the entire story of what had just occurred.

She began by saying that she had been praying, and someone came and ordered her to stop. When she resisted and continued to pray, she was taken away, beaten up, and dragged to the first basement, where she was put in a coffin with some other people.

Next, she said, while she was still there, I came with some other people. I later learned that when I went out for these rescue missions, other than Jesus, I was always accompanied by angels. I began to open the coffins and took the people out of them. Then we took them to a certain tent, where they were tied with a golden ribbon. The tent had so much light in it that Priscilla could not see who was tying the ribbon.

After that, I walked with all of them up some stairs that were made of fire, but they were not burning. After the stairs, we found a river of blood, where I led them through swimming in the river. Then we found Someone seated. She said, "You paraded us before the Person. The place was so bright that I could not see who it was. You prayed for us, and then we were freed, and I came home." This narration of what happened given by Priscilla really surprised me, and it continues to surprise me.

I went to this basement many times, and I still go there, if the Lord allows me to. For example: when I pray for a sick person (as you know, their sickness comes from the devil), I sometimes have to travel to Hell and get the person out. When this happens, invariably the person is healed.

Sometimes the demons would have a discussion, and the Lord would allow me to hear what they were talking about. Once, as they were talking, they said that since I had become such a troublemaker, they were going to kill and bury Priscilla so that when I went to Hell looking for her, I would not find her. After they finished talking, I "walked to Hell," but this time I was not looking for coffins, but, instead, for those who had been buried in the ground. The demons were very upset, and they asked each other, "Who told her what we did?"

Sometimes they had very bad plans for me, or for persons in my family or at my place of work, and the Lord would allow me to overhear their conversations. This way I would know how to pray and what to ask of the Lord. Even when people are planning evil concerning me or anything that concerns me, sometimes the Lord allows me to hear what they are talking about. I can't explain this, but it still happens.

Usually a basement in Hell has several areas where people are tormented. Once, when I went looking for

My Visits to Heaven and Hell

Priscilla, still in the first basement, I found people locked up in cells with very strong metal bars. The people in these places were wounded and could not even talk. After I got them out, they would just stand there like sheep. To get them to move, I literally had to push them. These were people who had lost hope, and the demons had tormented so much that even when help came, they could not see it and believe that it had come for sure. Notice that the Lord is present in every basement (see Job 26:6). *"If I ascend up into heaven, thou art there: if I make my bed in hell, behold, thou art there"* (Psalm 139:8).

The cells took different shapes and designs. Some of them were made of thick grills, while others had thin grills. Others were completely sealed, cream in color, while others were black. All the people in these areas were in bondage, and they could not move until they were pushed. What was surprising to me was that some of these people were prominent men and women, well-to-do people and those in places of authority.

I could actually identify very few of these people. When I asked the Lord who they were and why I only knew a few of them, He said that they were people from all over the world. The other very sad thing He told me about the many people I had rescued and brought before Him was that some of them would still go back. I remembered this when a woman came to me one day and asked me to help her pray for her sister, who was HIV positive. I spoke to the Lord about it that night. He told me that He was not going to heal the woman. When I asked Him why He was not going to heal her, He told me that He had already healed her once, but that she had gone back. He said that she was into prostitution, and after He had healed her, she went back to the same business.

I talked to Him about what the Bible says on forgiveness, but He still said He would not heal her. I asked Him what I should tell the sister. He said that I should tell her that we would continue praying. I said to Him, "Lord, won't that be a lie?" He said it wasn't a lie, so that's what I told her. The sick lady eventually died, so when the Lord says that some of the people that I rescued will go back, I understood. This lady had been healed, but she went back and got herself infected again.

In that same basement, I found a large tree farm. The trees there were planted by people who are still with us on earth. Remember that people who are in bondage are not necessarily dead already. The people working in the tree farms were people who are alive today, and as I had said before, they could be poor or rich and prominent people. Apart from Priscilla whom I found working on the tree farms, there were other people whom I knew, as well as many others whom I did not know.

The farms were on a hilly place. Each person had to go to the nursery and get a plant, and the nursery was down where there was a river. Once a person planted their trees, it was their responsibility to water them continually, and the water had to be brought from the river using containers. Satan cannot use irrigation, because his idea is to get people to work and keep on work, and to be tormented, until they cannot even think of anything better. At the same time that they do all this, they are assigned demons who beat them continually. It is never ending, and none of us would want our worst enemies to be in that place. It is a very bad place indeed.

Once the trees are ready for harvesting, they are cut down by a different set of people, who then turn them into lumber and transport them to the place where the coffins are made. The only work I saw being done with the lumber was to make coffins.

I know that other people have been to Hell, but according to what the Lord told me, Hell is a very big place, and some may have been there and not seen the tree farms, but that does not mean that they do not exist.

Keep in mind that I was still in the first basement. Hell goes on down to the twelfth basement, where you actually get to meet Satan himself. It was necessary for me to make this journey because I needed to rescue Priscilla.

After we came back, she would narrate (and thus confirm) everything that I had seen. All the time that I was in this basement I could still see the Lake of Fire, but the people that I was to rescue were not in the fire. Remember, these are not dead people, but living people whose lives are bound in Hell.

Although most of the things I saw can be described, some of the experiences I had cannot be explained in writing. I would like to share one that surprised me and may not make sense to others. Priscilla had travelled to her home in Tanzania, and one day, while she was there, some people paid her a visit. Just before they could leave, her sister was attacked by demons. She threw herself on the ground and started moving about like a snake. Then she began attacking the visitors and her family members. She needed to be delivered from those demons, and so Priscilla decided to cast out the demons the way she had seen me do it. She tried for more than two hours, but the demons did not leave her sister. Then she decided to call me for help.

Remember that she was in Tanzania, and I was in Kenya. She called and narrated what had happened. I asked her to continue praying and assured her that I would be praying too. I went into my prayer room and started praying, and to my surprise I suddenly found myself in the home of Priscilla's family in Tanzania. The sister was still on the floor, and Priscilla was standing by her side praying. Most of the visitors had left, and the other family members were waiting outside. I commanded the demons to come out of her sister in the name of Jesus Christ, and they obeyed and left. I stopped praying and called Priscilla back to see if what

My Visits to Heaven and Hell

I had experienced was happening. She confirmed that the demons had left.

This and other experiences are not easy to explain on paper. I know that we all want to hear about what is usual and what makes sense, but our God is not usual, and His ways are very different from ours. Even when you read the Bible, you will find many things that don't seem to make sense. The minute we want the things of God to be usual and to make sense, we are bringing Him down to our level of experience. It is our responsibility to move from our experience in order to find God. This way we will understand some of His ways.

Please note that I have said that we will understand *some* of God's ways. We can never fully understand God, but He allows us so much. The responsibility is on us to learn as much as we can about Him, which can never be enough. The more you think that you know God, the more you come to realize how little you know about Him. When you come to know God, you will begin to seek Him that you may know Him even better. Let me list a few experiences from the Bible that confirm further the "unusualness" of our God:

- At the Red Sea, water divided to form dry ground, with a wall of water on the right and another on the left (see Exodus 14:15-22). What can anyone make out of this experience? Our responsibility is to let God be God and allow ourselves to be used by Him. In that way, we can have some of His experiences.

Jesus said in John 14:12: *"Verily, verily, I say unto you, He that believeth on me, the works that I do shall he do also; and greater works than these shall he do; because I go unto my Father."* We have a responsibility, and we need to rise to the position that God has given us. We should be able, as believers, to do much more than Jesus Christ did. God is unusual, and you, too, can be unusual – if you have faith in God and allow yourself to be used by Him in whichever way He desires. I can tell you for sure that you will not be popular. If you want God to use you and bless you, you must be ready to be rejected and called names by your own family members and friends. I have experienced this. But those same people, before too long, will be looking for you. Take the example of Jesus. When He was on the cross, people mocked Him and called Him names, but those same people needed Him later. It may take a long time, but our God will always come through for you. There is no better place to be than at the feet of our Lord Jesus Christ.

- God fed the children of Israel with manna from Heaven (see Numbers 11:7-9). This was also not usual.

- The fall of Jericho (see Joshua 6). How does a wall collapse just because people have gone round it for six days and on the seventh day they go round it six times and on the seventh time trumpets sound and people shout? This is unusual and does not make sense. This is how our God works when we learn to trust in Him.
- An ax head floated (see 2 Kings 5:1-7). Elisha, the man of God, made an iron axe to float. This is against the Law of Gravity and other scientific laws. This is the God that I am talking about in this book, a God who cannot be stopped by anything, a God who is not usual, a God whose ways are many and different from ours. Amen!

- The death of Jesus (see Matthew 27:50-54). The tombs broke open, and the bodies of many holy people who had died were raised to life again. They came out of the tombs and, after Jesus Christ's resurrection, went into the Holy city and appeared to many people.

This God is the same yesterday, today and forever. He is capable of anything, and nothing can stop Him from doing what He has purposed to do in your life. Let us praise Him. Hallelujah! My brothers and sisters, we have hindered the Lord from blessing us because we have not allowed ourselves to know Him and to work with Him. I say this with confidence because I know the blessing with which He has blessed me. I also know the plans that He has for me, plans to prosper me. He told me that the devil's schemes will never stop Him from what He has in store for His children. Don't be bothered by what other people have. You never know where their rewards come from.

Satan does not give free gifts. Anything that he gives must be paid for by the recipient. People should be very careful in the way they acquire wealth. They should pray and work hard, do clean businesses, and live a holy life, and God will bless them according to His riches in glory. What God gives is blessed and permanent. The devil will destroy you by pretending that he has anything good to offer.

I say this without fear. I know that Satan hates me, and he did not want me to write this book. If anything, he would want me dead and never again able to speak about his ways to anyone. On the other hand, God loves me so much and wanted me to finish writing this book, so that the devil could be exposed. That is why God gave me these experiences, to let others know about our common enemy, Satan.

Chapter Six

The Twelve Basements of Hell

As I mentioned before, the Lord took me to both Heaven and Hell many times. This would happen as I went to look for Priscilla. These visits took place over a period of about three years.

Hell is a big place, with a lot of things happening. The Lord did not take me to the place where the dead are, but from where we would go, I could still see the big fire and people burning. On one occasion, in Hell, I met a man who was a devil worshiper. We fought until I overpowered him. I called fire down that burned him into ashes. I collected those ashes, put them in a container (a small metal box), and threw it in that big fire.

In this chapter, I would like to continue narrating my experiences in Hell. Remember that I would go there and come back the same day. Hell has twelve basements. This is what the Lord told me. In every basement, there are a lot of activities going on. In every basement there are demons on guard. They are very bad. They will beat up a person, even though that person is working and doing what is expected of him.

No one can do a good job, as far as the Satan is concerned. Anything you do for him deserves a punishment. The better you become, the worse he treats you. That is why, when he gives his gifts, he will ask for the sacrifice of a loved one. Do not take this information lightly. These things are happening, and they are here with us.

Satan does not fear size, status, money, or connections. He only fears the name of Jesus Christ. Seek Jesus that He may rescue you from the powers of Satan. If you fail to do this, Satan will recruit you to serve him and will finally destroy you and your loved ones.

What Happens in Hell's Basements?

1. The First Basement

In the first basement, people are put in coffins, as I explained in Chapter Five. There are so many coffins there that the human eye cannot see the end of them. In each coffin, there is more than one person, with some of the coffins having as many as four people in them. In these coffins, one does not breathe, and yet there is no death – just torment and intimidation.

Some of the coffins are buried under the ground. It took the Lord's hand for me to see those. When I found them, I would remove the people from them and help them meet Jesus. Please note that I have had to simplify what happens in the basements of Hell, for some experiences cannot be described in writing.

2. The Second Basement

In the second basement, people are in cells, with black grills, but they are not chained. They look so desperate and without hope. They are so tormented that even if help was to come, they would not recognize it. For me to get some of the people out of this place, I had to literally pull and push them out.

In the first and second basements, some people are working in a huge tree farm. This farm is on the side of a mountain. The people doing the planting are supervised by demons and are constantly being beaten and tormented. It is the responsibility of each person to go and collect their seedlings from the nursery, go fetch water from a river at the bottom of the mountain, and then come back up the mountain and plant their trees. It is a never-ending process.

Down in Hell there is no day. It's always dark, always night. In Hell, there are no peaceful moments. People are either being beaten by demons or are in pain for having to work around the clock. The people there have lost their dignity, for anything can happen to them at any time. There are no good moments. This is one of the things that make me want to talk about Jesus to everyone, everywhere, anytime. I would not want anyone to go to Hell, not even the most callous of my enemies. Hell is not meant for human beings, but for Satan and his demons. One goes to Hell by choice and not by design. Please preach Jesus to everyone, everywhere, anytime, so that we may rescue our people. Keep in mind that the people I am talking about in these basements are not dead. These are people who are still alive today.

3. The Third Basement

In the third basement, people are kept in completely sealed cells, and just by walking around you might not know that there were people there. They make no sound and no movements. Remember, these people, in reality, are not dead. They are alive and still with us. Occasionally I would meet someone I knew there, but this was very rare.

All the people confined in this third basement just sit and wait. They do not talk to one another. To them, it is as if each one of them is on his or her own. One can see the pain on their faces. They do not seem to be aware of their surroundings. Even in this basement, I had to pull and push people to get them out. Remember that all of this time Jesus was with me, although sometimes I did not seem to see Him. But the moment any trouble began, He would show up.

4. The Fourth Basement

In this basement was a very big hall full of women being raped by demons. The women were helpless, and there was total silence in the hall. These women were like dead people. They did not say a word as they went through their painful ordeals. When I got in these places, the Lord would place in me the love that He has for us, and I would become so angry about what was happening that I would take drastic measures. For instance, I remember that once I called for a sword and ordered that all the demons that were raping women be castrated. This was done. One of the demon leaders asked me what I expected them to do.

Some demons would be bold enough to come to me and ask why I was stopping them. They would tell me that this was their territory. At this, I would order fire to come down and burn them to ashes. After the rescues, I would use the same route I mentioned in earlier chapters and take the people to Jesus. He would bless them and allow them to go on with life.

5. The Fifth Basement

In this basement was another very big hall where men were being sodomized by demons. Again there was dead silence. Here I did the same thing as I had done in the fourth basement. All these basements

My Visits to Heaven and Hell

are places I would visit for many days, rescuing people and destroying demons. I did this until the Lord moved me to some other basement. As I have mentioned earlier, it took three years for me to get to the last basement, where Satan sits.

This experience was very important, as Jesus Christ wants people to be told about these places, so that they may seek Him and He may deliver them. He told me that some of the people I had removed from Hell would go back. This is very unfortunate, but it happens because of sin and mainly the love of money, which the Bible says is *"the root of all evil"* (1 Timothy 6:10). Most people will do just about anything to get money, even if it means selling their soul to Satan.

Many times Satan would send very powerful demons to market me for his kingdom. Remember that Satan knows your price tag. He knows what you are worth, and he purposes to stop you before you even begin. He will do anything to get you to his side. He knows that you will be a problem to his kingdom, if he does not stop you, because of the seed that God has put in you.

When Satan is working on you and trying to get you to join his team, he does not do it alone. He will use anybody that is available – no matter who it is. I am saying this with confidence because of the things that I heard and saw in Hell. This is when you begin to have very serious problems with everyone — your family members, your friends, and your employer (if in employment). If you are in business, your business almost stops. You begin taking huge losses, so that the mention of extra money to you will be very appealing.

My experience was very painful, and I would not want anyone to go through the same experience. But if the Lord allows you to experience something similar, then it is for your good. He will always be there for you, but I can assure you that there is a price to pay.

Satan came to me with a proposal. He said he would give me Kshs. 50,000 a day. To me, this was a lot of money, considering that I was having financial difficulties. Satan will work things out so that at the time he comes to you, you will be down in terms of finances or down in whatever else he wants to use to get you on his team. It could be sickness, and he promises healing. More often than not, he uses money.

Always remember that money is not the answer to your problems. Only Jesus has the solution to your problems. When Satan comes, he will not disclose to you what is in the situation for him. Another thing that Satan will do is to give you examples of people who are serving him and what he has done for them. The people he named to me were doing very well for themselves indeed, but when I went for my visits to Hell, I would find those same people experiencing a lot of problems. Some would be hanging upside down naked. Others would be suspended in the air with chains tied around their arms and legs. Their legs were spread apart, revealing their nakedness. These were people, in very senior positions in the world, would be alone in a cell with demons tormenting them. In the natural, these were people who seemed to be doing very well. And, again, I am speaking of people whom I knew. Please don't be cheated. Wait on God.

Let me warn anyone who is serving Satan. You have just a few years before you will go into eternal torment. Yes, you are enjoying life now, even though you are messing up with God's children, but woe unto you if you do not change your ways and seek God. He knows all that you are doing for Satan, and some of his children know too. Your sin is no secret, for Satan has no secrets. He tells others about you just, like he told me. When you are selling a product or service, you will give reference to the clients who are currently using your product. This is the same principle Satan uses, and he does it because it works.

My sister and my brother, reconsider your position and what you are going through now. You still have a chance. Think of your life now and your life after death, and change your loyalties. Come to Jesus Christ. He will rescue your life. I know that Satan has put a lot of fear in you, and you think that he owns your life. Believe me when I say he does not own your life. Forget about him and his threats. Once you are in Christ Jesus, Satan has no power over you. The devil is already defeated. He lost the battle a long time ago. He continues to use fear to woe the children of God.

Please don't bow to his threats. Just be encouraged and move on. Seek the Lord Jesus Christ, and you will see what God can do. If you are reading this book and you are a believer, please help others to know that Satan has no power over their lives. They can be free – if they seek God.

6. The Sixth Basement

In the sixth basement, there were a lot of different activities taking place. There was a big machine that grated people who continued to resist Satan. People were put into this machine alive. They were first forced into a pipe, which emptied them into the grating machine. After a person had been grated, they were given as food to a very old and powerful demon in the form of a woman. This demon had no teeth. She fed on human flesh, and was a special one in charge of the whole floor. The rest of the demons worked very hard to ensure that she got her food continuously.

When I got there, the Lord enabled me to destroy the machine and set the whole place on fire. I also burned and destroyed the demons that were operating the machine. I set the old demon in the form of a woman ablaze, too. This was a lot of work.

I thought that I had finished with the machine, when the Lord told me that there were many machines of that nature in the production department. He took me there, and for sure, I found many demons at work, busy producing more of this machine. There was a lot of material on site.

This machine was made of metals and it had very sharp blades or knives. I managed to destroy every job in progress and set on fire the building materials that were waiting to be assembled. To my surprise, after I had destroyed everything, the Lord told me that there were other machines in a shop in one of the countries. We went there, and I set the shop on fire, including the store.

7. The Seventh Basement

The entire floor of this basement is the back of a large snake that is constantly moving. The Lord had to suspend me over it for some time, until I could call down fire that burned the snake and left only ashes in its place. On this level, people were locked into large cells that were not visible from the outside, but with the Lord's help, I was able to notice the totally white sealed doors. I would call the people to come out, but most of them did not seem to understand what I was doing. In fact, most of them seemed to have lost their minds. The leaders, who were people doing very well in the world were there hanging upside down or suspended in the air with chains about them. All these leaders were usually naked and in more pain than the people they led. According to Satan, when you serve him, you suffer more. This is the true reward for serving Satan.

Most of the people I rescued, according to Jesus, will be saved, but others will choose to go back to Hell. For all of us who are saved, someone rescued us. Five years prior to my travel to Hell, the Lord had spoken to me and told me that He would give me a job of cleaning His children. At the time, I did not understand what this meant and how involving it would be. I desired to serve the Lord so much that what He asked of me was always answered with a yes. To date, my answer to serve the Lord is more than just a mere yes. I love the Lord so much that I am ready to serve Him at any cost.

I thank God for His faithfulness and am happy to say that I know what it means to serve God. I also know that it takes God's help for anyone to serve Him. We need to surrender our lives to Jesus one hundred percent if He is to use us. Please note: the greater your responsibility, the more intense His dealings with you will be. We need to understand that those whom He calls must be refined and trained by the Holy Spirit in the school of tests and trials (see Psalm 11:5).

8. The Eighth Basement

I found a similar snake in this basement to the one in the seventh basement, but this one was wounded, with a deep cut on the back that was still bleeding. The back of the snake was like a big river of blood. The snake was still moving and covering the whole place so that I could not see the ground. I had to be suspended to call on the fire of the Lord Jesus Christ to burn the snake and give me access to the ground. On this level, people were packed into containers the size of a lift or elevator. They were so tightly packed that breathing was a problem.

The entire floor was covered with these invisible containers, and one could easily have thought that there were no people in the area. Remember that I was going to all these places because I needed to rescue Priscilla, and I did not know exactly where she was. I would eventually find her in one of these containers, and when we got back home, she would narrate the story of what had happened and where I found her.

9. The Ninth Basement

In this floor, the torment continued. People were in drawers, must like a chest of drawers. They were so big that they could accommodate many people, some up to six. When I found these people, they would be like dead people, although they were still alive. They would be packed in there like cloths, and they would be in such terrible agony that they did not talk or make any noise at all. They had gone through so much pain that there was no longer any point in trying to cry out.

Here, again, these drawers were hidden, and there was no movement. On every floor, there were demons tormenting the victims.

10. The Tenth Basement

On this level, the demons were having a field day. There was a big pot and it was boiling with cooking oil. The pot was so big that it could take about five people at a time. It was meant for deep frying human beings. The demons use forks to poke the people and force them deeper into the boiling oil. This was just to torment them, since demons would be more interested in raw human flesh with blood than in anything deep fried.

Even though these people were put into boiling oil, they did not die. I would find Priscilla in the queue. In some cases she would just be about to be put into the boiling oil when I got there.

11. The Eleventh Basement

I had a very bad experience on this floor. When I got there, I found demons seated at a large round table eating babies that were still alive. They would plunge their long, hard nails into the baby's body, pull out the heart and eat it. The feasting demons were many, and the babies would be placed on the table like we do at platters of food mealtime. While every demon was holding a baby, there were other babies on the table, waiting for their turn to be eaten. Each demon would be expected to eat many babies. When I saw what was happening, the Lord empowered me to call fire down and destroy all the demons on that site and to turn everything upside down, including the tables.

I also discovered a store on this floor that had thousands of children from 2 to 5. The Lord told me that they were children of the world. That day I was able to rescue about a thousand of them. Even now, as you read this book, there are still very many children in that store. I continued going to this basement, to rescue more children, until the Lord moved me to the twelfth basement.

Just one day before I was able to deliver the manuscript for this book to the printer for the first edition, the Lord woke me up and told me to insert this vital information. You will notice that in all of the basements, after the Lord had blessed the people, they were released and allowed to come back to earth and to their homes. This does not happen with the eleventh floor basement, and the reason is that these children have nowhere to go. They do not have homes. This was the reason the Lord led me to build a children's home and sanctuary for them. He told me that, while everybody else left after He had blessed them, the children stayed on. He said that I should tell people about the children's home and let them know that this children's home was not like any other in the world. He said that He Himself would provide these children they would be children "without a claim." If I told God's children about this children's home, He said, they would be willing to contribute toward the upbringing of such children, and He told me to attach a form that would allow His people to partner with Him in bringing these children up.

He said to me: "Tell My people that those who will partner with me in bringing up these children, I the Lord will partner with them in all that they do." Today you can be a beneficiary of what the Lord has said. Please go to the last page of this book and sign the attached form and mail it to me and become a beneficiary. If you have a relative or a friend who would like to be part of what the Lord is doing, you may make copies of the form and have them sign and mail it to me.

The Lord is saying, "I always intervene when you put My agenda before yours and go for it. At that moment, Heaven sends angels, resources, strength, and the people you need."

12. The Twelfth Basement

This is the last floor, where you meet Satan himself. While in the fifth basement, the demons there told me that the basements only went down to the seventh basement, but Jesus told me that is was a lie, that I needed to go down to the twelfth basement.

Some of the things I saw on this level cannot be put into writing. On this floor, one lands on a very small opening. The rest of the space is filled with Satan himself. He presents himself as a big snake.

My Visits to Heaven and Hell

When I arrived at this level, I became very frightened because on one wall was the opened mouth of Satan, ready to swallow me up. He would like some of us dead. Many times he has asked me to stop talking to people about Jesus. He has called me names and issued a lot of threats, but those threats land on deaf ears. When you know your God, nothing can shake you. Satan has sent his people — real people and demons — to try to frustrate me on all fronts. But they always get defeated in the name of Jesus Christ.

When I talk of real people, I mean real people. When Satan decides to work on you, he will use anything and everything and anyone and everyone. I am speaking out of experience. The good thing is that the more he attacks you, the more Jesus becomes real in your life. I have had some very interesting battles, some of them physical and others spiritual, and in all of them the Lord has given me victory. Of course, this victory did not come without pain. There is a price to pay for ministry, for this I have many witnesses, servants of God who have had to pay the price that I am talking about.

In the twelfth basement of Hell, at the side of the mouth of Satan were many smaller snakes that grew and attempted to pull me into his mouth. At that moment, the Lord helped me to remember that I could call for back-up, and I did. Four angels immediately came with drawn swords. Even though the snakes kept growing, they were trimmed by the angels until finally I was able to overpower Satan. However, this fight took months, and as the angels trimmed the growing snakes, I could see Priscilla inside the mouth of the biggest snake.

While I was still in the twelfth basement, when I finally overpowered Satan, I got inside through his mouth. To my surprise, every space between the bones of the snake was a door leading to very large hall where there were people filled with torment, fear, and frustration. I spent many days rescuing these people.

This basement required more of my time than all the others. After I had fought with Satan for many days, the Lord enabled me to establish a rescue room that was like a church. Anytime I would rescue people, I would bring them into this big hall, and the Lord would bless them and empower them to be able to travel with me back to earth, as I described in Chapter Five. Notice that the Lord was present in every basement of Hell, just as He is in Heaven. This confirms to us that our God is omnipresent.

From this basement there were a few steps that we would climb, and then we would be lifted up.

Most of the people in this place were tormented more than on any other floor. Satan knows our price tag, and for that reason, he will keep people very far from their calling. It takes the hand of God to move and rescue His people. God wants to involve you and me in doing this work, and that is why He allows us to have these kinds of experiences, so that we may be a blessing to others.

May the Lord God help you to believe what He made me go through for the sake of many others of God's children, because what I have written is true and from God Himself. Be encouraged and know that God wants the best for you and for me. Pray for all people of the world — parents, brothers, sisters, children, neighbors, and any other person the Lord may bring to your remembrance. The human race is in so much trouble because the devil knows his time is very limited. I am writing this because the Lord wants you to know, so that you may do something with the information. Please do something. The Lord wants this book to awaken believers to know that they need to pray and protect others. Our God is righteous, and there are things that He will not do for us until we pray, or someone prays for us.

These visits to the basements of Hell might appear strange to the reader, but this is what happens when we pray for non-believers or a demonized person for deliverance. This is the ministry that the Lord has called me to, and, indeed, all ministers of the Gospel. The difference between my experience and that of other ministers who have not had this type of experience is that the Lord allowed me to see what happens when we pray. Of course, He does not allow us to see it with our natural eyes.

I want to believe that there are other ministers who may have had my kind of experience. This happens in the Spirit realm, and only God chooses who is to experience it. One thing I know: this kind of experience was for the purpose of this book and for His other purposes which I may not yet know. When we say that people are bound, this is what it means. When we pray for people with problems, they are released from different levels of bondage (the various basements). The levels depend on several issues, but the two main issues are: (1) The call that person has, what God has put in them. A call can make the devil lock a person away as far as possible in one of his basements. (2) The other thing is the level of involvement with the powers of darkness. The devil's thinking is that such a person may never get out of bondage, and that is why believers should pray for non-believers without growing weary. It is only through prayer that we can overturn Satan's strategies and gain victory. Amen!

Before I close this section, I want to insert two recent testimonies:

A Testimony from Amelia Tyson

One day I was walking my dog down a local road, and as I did so, I was singing a praise-and-worship song and overflowing with the joy of the Lord. Suddenly I looked up and saw a huge man walking in the middle of the street toward me with his arms crossed and a very haughty

My Visits to Heaven and Hell

look on his face. I could barely believe what I was seeing. This man was taller than any man I had ever seen, and he didn't look normal. He must have been at least ten feet tall.

When I saw him, I immediately stopped. He was still a good distance from me, at least three car lengths. When he finally saw me, he immediately turned in the other direction and ran yelling. He seemed very afraid of me.

For a moment, I stood frozen in my tracks. Fear tried to grip me. I looked down, and my dog's tail was between her legs. She could probably sense my fear. I'm not sure if she saw what I did or not. Then God spoke to my heart and told me that this had been no ordinary man, but rather a demon, and that he had been afraid of me because God's power and glory were within me as His child.

I was still in shock as the man reached the other end of the block and then disappeared. There was nowhere for him to go, for there the road came to an abrupt dead-end. There, at the end of that road, is a famous cemetery surrounded by a very tall iron fence and gate. I walked to the end of the block and turned to the left and to the right, but there was nobody. The man had simply vanished.

As God spoke to my heart, I felt a bit better, but the whole thing was still very shocking. The truth is that the spirit realm is just as real as what you and I see on a daily basis. I believe God allowed me to see that huge demon run from me to give me a great connection with the scriptures that say:

Greater is he that is in you, than he that is in the world. 1 John 4:4

Be sober, be vigilant; because your adversary the devil, as a roaring lion, walketh about, seeking whom he may devour: whom resist stedfast in the faith.
1 Peter 5:8-9

A Testimony from Emily Stanfield

During my visit to the ___ basement, I encountered people who were shackled in chains. It is important to remember that those people are also physically alive and busy with their daily activities in the earth. However, they are also in suffering and in bondage and can discern what is happening in their lives.

During my recent visit to the U.S., I met and prayed with a lady by the name of Emily Stanfield in North Carolina who, in a recent e-mail to me, had this to say regarding her bondage:

For a while now, I have felt the enemy's counterfeit power in my mouth and around my chest and heart. I have also felt shackles around my hands and feet and a yoke around my neck as I walk. I can sense them and see them with my spiritual eyes."

Most people know that there is something wrong with their lives, but do not know where to go to get help. Our assignment is to pray that the Holy Spirit quickens us in prayer for these people to let the Lord release and rescue them from their bondage. The Son of God, Jesus, was manifested to destroy the works of Satan in people's lives. Let us pray for people, so that we can give Jesus access into their lives, to set them free. Jesus came to set the captives free, and it is for freedom that we have been set free.

After I prayed for Emily, I received a testimony from her that the Lord had delivered her, and she was in sound mind and praising God for His wonderful work in her life. Amen!

Chapter Seven

Handwritten Messages from Jesus

The Lord asked me to buy some writing materials. He said that He would be writing messages for me, and every day of my training I would find written messages on paper, which the Lord told me to keep secure. These messages are still available in black and white. I will include fourteen of them in this book. They are, however, not in the order in which they were written. I have since typed them, and I use them for teaching as the Lord allows. To me this is such a great miracle.

Our God is faithful. Once, when I was still a young believer, He asked me to start a fellowship at my place of work. Just as with others the Lord calls, I had very good reasons why God could not use me. I told Him that I did not know the Bible, and therefore I would not be able to share about Him with others. I had bought my first Bible after I got saved, and now the Lord asks me, of all people, to start a fellowship.

My Visits to Heaven and Hell

I found it very difficult and, for sure, I did not know where to start.

Secondly, there were other people in my office who where better placed because they had been saved for many years. I felt inadequate, and I thought that the Lord was going to excuse me and give the assignment to someone who had been saved longer. However, the Lord told me that when I started the fellowship He would tell me what to say. For two years, after I obeyed and started the fellowship, He gave me messages every time I had a meeting. This is a long story, but it is what brought about the written messages six years later. Because of His faithfulness and the fact that I had told Him that I did not know what to say, He still gives me messages today.

Some of the messages God has given me are in Kiswahili, and others are in English. I will include only some of the English messages here.

Message No. 1:

Confessions and the Transferrables

Ask the Holy Spirit to reveal to you every sin in your life. As He does so, write them down on a sheet of paper. Quite likely, your list will include among many others items:

- Jealousy
- Pride
- Selfishness
- Lust
- Indifference to the things of God
- Loss of first love and many others

After you have completed your list, write out this wonderful promise:

If we confess our sins, he is faithful and just to forgive us our sins, and to cleanse us from all unrighteousness. 1 John 1:9

Realize that this list is just between you and God, so be completely honest. Tell God everything that is wrong. When you have completed your time of

My Visits to Heaven and Hell

prayer, destroy the list. Before you do so, however, express your gratitude to the Lord that He has forgiven you through what Christ did on the cross about two thousand years ago. Remember that faith is not tears, pleading, or any other self-imposed spiritual discipline. It lays hold of God's promise to forgive and cleanse us from all sin.

This is not a new or second forgiveness. You are simply realizing in your experience the once-and-for-all forgiveness which we read about in the book of Hebrews chapter 10. Some confession will also involve restitution, returning something which you have stolen or asking another whom you have wronged to forgive you. This is vitally important because you cannot maintain a clear conscience before God if you still have a guilty conscience before your fellow man. At the conclusion of a Christian medical meeting where I spoke on this subject of forgiveness, one of the doctors present accepted my challenged to go and make his list. He was very excited when he came to see me the next morning. "Last night, about midnight," he said, "a doctor friend of mine came to me and said that for years, while pretending to be my friend, he had actually hated me. He was making his own list, and the Lord told him that he must come and ask my forgiveness. We had a most wonderful time of prayer together, and God met us in a special way. I wanted to tell you this to encourage you to keep teaching Christians to confess their sins to God, and, if necessary, to ask forgiveness from those they have wronged, as the Holy Spirit leads them."

God has a wonderful, abundant, fruitful life planned for us, but He will not bless us or use us until we face up to this problem of sin. He is holy and righteous, eternally aflame with the glory of perfection, and wants us in our experience to be all that He has created us to be. His plan is that we be changed into the image of His dear Son. This can never be our experience if we refuse to acknowledge and confess our sins.

A young man once said to me, after an evening meeting, "I did not believe I needed to make a list. I could not think of anything seriously wrong in my life. But when I saw others making their lists, the Spirit of God told me to do it as well." He concluded, "While there were no serious problems, there were a lot of little things, and the sum total of the little things had dulled the cutting edge of my witness for Christ. If ever you speak on this subject again, be sure to insist that everyone – including those who think there is no sin in their lives – make such a list. Had I not made my list, I would have missed a blessing from God."

It may be that there are no gross sins in your life, but if your heart is cold toward God, you are lacking in faith, you are not fruitful, like the churches of Ephesus and Laodicea referred to in Revelation 3, you have lost your first love for the Lord, or are lukewarm, there is something wrong. Tell God about it. I suggest that you pause right now, take a pencil and paper and list every sin in your life which the Holy Spirit calls to your remembrance. Take plenty of time and humble yourself before the Lord. Give Him time to reveal to you those areas of your life which need to be corrected.

When you have written down all that is shown to you, write across the list the wonderful promise of 1 John 1:9: *"If we confess our sins, he is faithful and just to forgive us our sins, and to cleanse us from all unrighteousness."* Now, thank God for His forgiveness and cleansing through the shedding of His Son's precious blood for Your sins. If you have confessed all your known sins, any guilt complex reminding you of those sins will be from Satan, for God has forgiven all your sins on the basis of Christ's death on the cross for you (see Hebrews 10:1-7).

Now thank God for what He has promised. Your sins have been removed as far as the east is from the west. They are buried in the deepest sea. God has put them behind His back and remembers them against you no more. Think of it! God has forgiven you! God loves you!

The list of your sins is strictly between you and the Lord. Be sure to destroy it as soon as you have confessed them to God. You can be assured, without question, that today you experience forgiveness and cleansing for all the sins of the past. Through the principle of spiritual breathing you can get off of the spiritual roller coaster and stay off for the rest of your life.

Christ came to seek and to save the lost. He has commissioned us to go and bring forth the fruits, but He will not bless us and use us to bring others to Himself if there is unconfessed sin in our lives. Trust Christ Jesus now for a total supernatural forgiveness and cleansing of all your sins, and enter into the great adventure for which He created you.

The Transferrables

All that ever came before me are thieves and robbers: but the sheep did not hear them. I am the door: by me if any man enter in, he shall be saved, and shall go in and out, and find pasture. The thief cometh not, but for to steal, and to kill, and to destroy: I am come that they might have life, and that they might have it more abundantly. John 10:8-10

A strategy to help change the world:

- How to experience God's love and forgiveness.
- How to be filled with the Spirit.
- How to walk in the Spirit.
- How to witness in the Spirit.
- How to love by faith.
- How to pray.

Make the concept, "How to experience God's love and forgiveness" a way of life through practicing the following:

My Visits to Heaven and Hell

- Set aside twenty to thirty minutes to be alone with God. Prayerfully ask Him to reveal to you any sinful attitude or actions that are displeasing to Him.
- Confess these sins and agree with God concerning them.
- Ask God daily to make you sensitive to anything in your life which would be displeasing to Him.
- Then, throughout the day, as you become aware of such an area, immediately pray and claim God's forgiveness according to His promise.
- Share this vital truth with other people as often as you can throughout the week.

The Conclusion

Remember any feelings of guilt that come your way, reminding you of sins committed before the list, is from the devil. Remind him that he is a liar and the father of all lies and that he is a defeated devil. Don't allow him to put you down. Remember, you are a child of a King. You are more than a conqueror, and the devil knows that (see John 8:44 and Romans 8:37)!

Message No. 2

Study Guide

Read the Bible or listen to a tape or cassette recording of it for six consecutive days. Educational research has shown that it is necessary to read or hear a concept six to ten times in order to understand it thoroughly. This is known as internalization. As you apply the principles presented in this concept, the joy of experiencing the cleansed life will become a way of life for you. A thorough understanding of this concept will enable you to communicate it more effectively to others.

Memorize the following verses and references:

I am come that they might have life, and that they might have it more abundantly. John 10:10

If we confess our sins, he is faithful and just to forgive us our sins, and to cleanse us from all unrighteousness. 1 John 1:9

Your memory work will be easier and more lasting if you will review it daily for the entire week rather than try to complete all of it in just one day. Also, review the verses memorized with previous concepts.

My Visits to Heaven and Hell

a) Study the taught questions. Before you answer any questions you must understand the question first.

b) Participate in a group discussion using the taught questions. If you are not already a part of a Bible study or action group which is studying the transferable concepts, you can form your own group by inviting others to join you in this study program. As you discuss the taught questions, share what God is teaching you about His love and forgiveness and share ideas regarding how you plan to apply this teaching in your life and how you plan to share it with others.

c) Finally, make this concept, "How to experience God's love and forgiveness," a way of life through practicing the following:

d) Set aside twenty to thirty minutes to be alone with God. Prayerfully ask Him to reveal to you any sinful attitude or actions of your life that are displeasing to Him and make a written list of them. Confess these sins and agree with God concerning them, according to His promise in 1 John 1:9. Across the list, write out the verse. Thank Him, according to His promise, and then destroy the list.

e) Ask God daily to make you sensitive to anything in your life which would be displeasing to Him. Then, throughout the day, as you become aware of such an area, immediately pray and claim God's forgiveness, according to His promise.

f) Use the brief outline below, the amplified outline, or a tape recording of the concept, to share this vital truth with other people. Share it as often as you can throughout the week. Provide a booklet and perhaps a tape or cassette for those with whom you share the concept, so that they, too, can study this material in depth and pass it on to others.

Amplified Outline

1. Knowing Jesus Christ personally is the greatest adventure man can experience:
   - Jesus Christ of Nazareth is the most remarkable, powerful, attractive personality of all the centuries (see Isaiah 7:14 and 53:4-6).
   - Jesus Christ meant for the Christian life to be an exciting, abundant adventure (see John 10:10 and Galatians 5:22-23).
   - Unfortunately, most Christians are not experiencing a life of joy and victory as taught in the Bible by the apostle Paul and our Lord (see Romans 5:3, 1 Thessalonians 5:18 and John 15:8).
   - The average Christian is not fruitful.
   - There is a vast difference between the Christianity of the New Testament and the Christianity evidenced in the lives of many Christians today.
   - The first-century church made a mighty impact for God upon the world.

My Visits to Heaven and Hell

And when they found them not, they drew Jason and certain brethren unto the rulers of the city, crying, these that have turned the world upside down are come hither also. Acts 17:6

- They knew the reality of being filled with the Spirit.
- They had met God's requirements of supernatural cleansing from their sins (see Psalm 51:2, 3, 10, 12 and 13).

2. Today we are greatly challenged as we face the most desperate hour of all human history:
   - The entire world is filled with anxiety, fear and frustration.
   - Never before in recorded history has there been such an ideal opportunity for presenting the claims of Christ.
   - In the midst of these tremendous problems and opportunities, most Christians have become more a part of the problem than of the solution.
   - They do not evidence a quality of life which causes others to want to know our Lord.
   - They do not know how to appropriate God's power and resources for making an impact in the world. The fact that many Christians are part of the problem rather than part of the solution can best be understood if we realize that there are three kinds of people in the world (see 1 Corinthians 2:14 and 3:3).

Natural man

There is the natural man who is not a Christian. He depends solely upon his own resources. Spiritually, he is dead to God – dead in trespasses and sins.

Spiritual man

There is the spiritual man, who is a Christian and who is controlled and empowered by the Holy Spirit of God. He draws continually upon the unlimited resources of God's love and power. Spiritually, he is alive to God, for the Son of God is living in and through Him. He brings glory to God because of his fruitful life.

Carnal man

There is the carnal man, who, though Christian, is trying to live in his own strength (see 1 Corinthians 3). He is a defeated and fruitless Christian. He never allows the Holy Spirit to mold him into the kind of person God created him to be. He lives in endless frustration. Sadly, he is often a person who does not realize that he is in the carnal category (see Romans 7:14-19). He lives in slavery to sin (see Romans 7:20-25).

God has provided the solution for the carnal Christian through the power of the Holy Spirit, who is able to liberate him from the vicious power of sin and death (see Romans 7:25 and 8:3). Self-imposed religious disciplines lead only to defeat and frustration. By faith, we can experience Christ's resurrection power and life in and through us (see Colossians 3:10, 1 Peter 1:7 and Hebrews 11:6).

Faith is another word for trust, but trust must have an object. The object of the Christian's faith is God and His Word (see John 14:14). It is tragic that the average Christian is a practical atheist — professing to believe in God, yet acting as though God either does not exist or is unwilling to help him.

An Abundant Life

Three Kinds of People

In 1 Corinthians 2-3, the apostle Paul, writing under the inspiration of the Holy Spirit, correctly diagnosed the problem when he tells us that there are three kinds of people in the world – the natural man, the spiritual man and the carnal man. If you are a defeated, frustrated, fruitless, impotent Christian, I have good news for you. Observe carefully what Paul has to say. You and every person alive on this planet can be identified in one of these three categories.

Natural Man

This is not a Christian. He depends upon his own resources and lives on his own strengths. He cannot understand or accept the truths of God's Word. His interests and ambitions are centered in things fleshy and worldly. Spiritually, he is dead to God – dead in trespasses and sin.

Spiritual Man

This is a Christian who is controlled and empowered by the Holy Spirit of God. He draws upon the unlimited resources of God's love and power, and lives in the strength of the living Christ. He understands and believes God's Word. His interests and ambitions are centered around and subject to the perfect will of God. Spiritually, he is alive. He is rejoicing in the Lord and bearing fruit for our Savior because he is allowing the Holy Spirit to have unhindered control over his life.

Carnal Man

The carnal man is a defeated and fruitless Christian. He is living in the energy of the flesh instead of drawing upon the inexhaustible resources of the Holy Spirit. He may be a Sunday school teacher, a salesman, a student or even a minister or missionary, who, even though he is a Christian, he is in control of his own life – wanting to be his own master and hoping to please Christ at the same time. He desires and sometimes attempts to set his affection on the things of this world. He may assume that he knows what God wants him to be and honestly try to live up to that self-made standard, only to fail again and again, because of rebellion, lack of information or lack of faith. He never allows the Holy Spirit to mold him into the person that God created him to be. Thus, in endless frustration, he lives outside the perfect will of God.

Somebody Else

Most Christians, whether or not they realize it, are in this carnal category. One man said to me, "I didn't know I was carnal. I have heard my pastor talk about carnal Christians, but I always thought he meant somebody else, who, I hoped, was hearing the pastor's message. Now, after hearing your message, I realize that I, too, am carnal." A businessman came to see me one day, greatly distressed because his church was splitting. "Half of our members are going to move out and start another church," he said. This distressed me too. I cannot think of anything more tragic than for a body of Christians to be divided.

As we talked, the man admitted that he was a carnal Christian. I began to explain that God had made a provision for him to be a spiritual person. He did not need to continue to live as a carnal Christian. Finally, we knelt together and prayed. He asked for forgiveness for his sins and asked God to fill and control his life by the Holy Spirit. As we were rejoicing over what God had done, he said, "You know, there won't be any problems in my church now. You see, I am the one who has been causing all the trouble."

To know Jesus Christ personally as Savior and Lord is the greatest privilege and adventure that man can ever experience. Jesus of Nazareth is invariably recognized as the most remarkable, the most powerful and the most attractive personality of all the centuries.

The date on your morning newspaper gives witness to the fact of His influence in history – AD, meaning Anno Domini, in the year of our Lord, and BC, meaning Before Christ. No other life since the beginning of time has so influenced for good the lives of so many multitudes of men and women. Hundreds of years before His birth, prophets of Israel had foretold His coming. These prophecies were fulfilled in the life of Jesus Christ, down to the very last detail:

- His miraculous birth
- His life
- His miracles
- His teachings
- His death on the cross for the sins of man
- And His resurrection.

He claimed to be the promised Messiah, the Son of God, and those who knew Him best died the death of martyrs, telling the Good News of God's visit to this planet through Jesus of Nazareth, to express His love and forgiveness for all mankind. Jesus Christ meant for the Christian life to be an exciting, abundant adventure. He said, *"I am come that they might have life, and that they might have it more abundantly"* (John 10:10). Christ's life gives us love, joy, peace, patience, kindness, faithfulness and goodness. A Christ-centered person is empowered by the Holy Spirit, introduces others to a new life, introduces others to prayer life, and understands God's

Word, trusts the teachings of the Kingdom and knows how to obey God in abundance — to the full, until it overflows.

When we walk in the fullness and control of God's Holy Spirit, every day is filled with wonder, meaning, purpose and fruitfulness. A rich and satisfying life is the heritage of every Christian:

> *But the fruit of the Spirit is love, joy, peace, longsuffering, gentleness, goodness, faith, meekness, temperance: against such there is no law.* Galatians 5:22-23

But most Christians do not know anything about this kind of life, a life of victory, joy and abundant fruitfulness for our Savior. On the contrary, to many people, the Christian life is a burden, a chore, hard work and a terrible cross to bear. They point to our Savior's infamous trial, brutal beatings and humiliating death on a cruel Roman cross and to the tens of thousands, even millions of Christian martyrs throughout the centuries. But a rich and satisfying life is the heritage of every Christian.

Message No. 3

I Do What I Hate

For we know that the law is spiritual: but I am carnal, sold under sin. For that which I do I allow not: for what I would, that do I not; but what I hate, that do I. If then I do that which I would not, I consent unto the law that it is good. Now then it is no more I that do it, but sin that dwelleth in me. For I know that in me (that is, in my flesh) dwelleth no good thing: for to will is present with me; but how to perform that which is good I find not. For the good that I would I do not: but the evil which I would not, that I do. Now if I do that I would not, it is no more I that do it, but sin that dwelleth in me. I find then a law, that, when I would do good, evil is present with me. For I delight in the law of God after the inward man: but I see another law in my members, warring against the law of my mind, and bringing me into captivity to the law of sin which is in my members. O wretched man that I am! Who shall deliver me from the body of this death? I thank God through Jesus Christ our Lord. So then with the mind I myself serve the law of God; but with the flesh the law of sin. Romans 7:14-25

My Visits to Heaven and Hell

Does this passage of scripture describe your present relationship with God? We should search ourselves. A gifted young educator, with his doctorate, a successful career and an even brighter future, came for counseling and confessed to me: "I became a Christian years ago when I was a young man. But through the years, I gradually took back the control of my life. I was still active in the church, in fact, in the biggest church in the city. Yet I am ashamed to say that I have been more interested in promoting my own business and social position than I have been in serving the Lord and getting to know Him better. I have compromised my business and professional standards and have not always been honest and ethical in my dealings with others."

"God has shown me that I am a carnal Christian and has reminded me of the many years I have wasted living selfishly for my own interests," he said. "I have come to confess my sins to God and surrender my life completely and irrevocably to Christ. Please pray for me that I may be a man of God and a spiritual Christian and not the carnal Christian that I have been all of these years. Now I want to volunteer for the great commission army and help evangelize the world for Christ."

Living by the Book

Another friend, one of the most dedicated men I have ever known, lived by a little black book. This book told the story of a life of extreme discipline. In this book, he kept a careful record of all of his activities – past, present and future. In it, he recorded:

- The time he was to get up every morning.
- How long to have his devotions.
- How many verses of scripture he should memorize that day.
- And to how many people he should witness.

I was very impressed. I wanted to be like him. However, one day he had a mental breakdown. After he was released from the hospital, he said to me, "I was unable to live the Christian life. I tried to be a man of God by imposing upon myself certain rigid spiritual disciplines. Before they took me to the hospital, my last conscious act was to throw that little black book, which had become my god, into the corner. I never wanted to see it again." My friend was trying to live for God in the energy of the flesh.

A Changed Attitude

A minister of a large church came to one of our institutes for evangelism. After my message on: "How to experience God's love and forgiveness," he came to talk to me. He was filled with hatred and resentment for the lay leaders of a church at which he had formerly served as a pastor. "These people did to me great harm," he said, "They tried to destroy me. I tried to get even with them, and as a result, I now realize that I have become a mean, critical, carnal Christian. Either I must get right with God or get out of the ministry. Every time I preach the Gospel, my words come back to condemn me. Pray for me that God will deliver me from this hatred, this cancerous carnality that is destroying my life and ministry."

A few days later he went to visit those hated church leaders. He told them that he loved them and asked them to forgive him. The leaders responded to him with love and forgiveness. They embraced each other with joy and Christian love. This dear pastor returned to his church with a heart of love that burned with zeal for our Lord. His ministry was revolutionized.

War Within

Paul continued his description of the carnal Christian:

> *Now if I do that I would not, it is no more I that do it, but sin that dwelleth in me. I find then a law, that, when I would do good, evil is present with me. For I delight in the law of God after the inward man: But I see another law in my members, warring against the law of my mind, and bringing me into captivity to the law of sin which is in my members. O wretched man that I am! who shall deliver me from the body of this death?*   Romans 7:20-25

Upon reading this, one of my friends said, "That's my biography, the story of my life." Have you ever asked this question in your own words, "Who will free me from my slavery to this deadly lower nature?"

The Great Solution

Every Christian has this same problem, until he makes the discovery that Paul made — that Jesus Christ our Lord has set him free. So there is now no condemnation awaiting those who belong to Jesus Christ (see Romans 8:1) through the power of the life-giving Spirit. And this power is mine through Christ Jesus. Jesus Christ has freed me from the vicious circle of sin and death.

We are not saved from sin's grasp by knowing the commandments of God, because we can't and we don't keep them. But God put into effect a different plan to save us. He sent His own Son in a human body like ours, except that ours is sinful and destroyed. He can exercise control over us because He gave Himself as a sacrifice for our sins.

How well I remember the years that I sought God with all my heart. I resorted to all kinds of self-imposed discipline, begging God for His power. The more I tried, the more defeated and frustrated I became. Then one day as I was studying the book of Romans, I read chapter 8 verse 7: *" Because the carnal mind is enmity against God: for it is not subject to the law of God, neither indeed can be."* What a relief it was for me to discover that

My Visits to Heaven and Hell

I would never be able to live the Christian life through my own efforts, but I could trust Christ to live His resurrection life in and through me. He alone could enable me to live the Christlife. It is faith, not effort, that pleases Him. Thank God! It has been done by Jesus Christ, our Lord! He has set me free!

Message No. 4

Proof of Discipleship

The average Christian is not fruitful. There is no better way than being fruitful, however, according to Christ's own words, to prove that we are His disciples. It is not enough to live a good life. Those who subscribe to other religions and cults which deny the deity of our Lord often live exemplary lives. An atheist can memorize prayers and wear a pious facade, falsely showing a feeling of deep respect for God, and do everything else that the average Christian does — as has been dramatically demonstrated in certain countries where Christianity is discouraged or banned, and informers have infiltrated the church even in positions of leadership, but for purpose of spying.

It is here that we discern a vast difference between the church of the New Testament and the church of today. The book of Acts of the Apostles tells the thrilling story of what God did through those first-generation Christians, as they went door to door sharing their faith — constrained by the love of Christ, often in the face of death and martyrdom. They went everywhere, as the apostle Paul said, telling everyone about Christ. This is seldom the experience of twenty-first century Christians.

In his preface to the young church in action, J.B. Phillips writes, "No one can read this book [of Acts] without being convinced that there is someone here at work besides mere human beings." Perhaps it was because of their very simplicity or perhaps because of their readiness to believe, to obey, to give, to suffer, and, if need be, to die.

The Spirit of God found what surely He must always be seeking — a fellowship of men and women so united in love and faith that He could work with them and through them with a minimum of hindrance. Consequently, it is a matter of sober historical fact that never before has any small body of ordinary people so moved the world that their enemies could say, with tears of rage in their eyes, that these men *"have turned the world upside down"* (Acts 17:6). Christians of that first century, filled with the Spirit and constrained by the love of God, took the Good News of God's love and forgiveness in Christ to the entire then known world — literally.

The Influence of Spiritual Christians

Why was that first-century church able to make an impact for God upon a wicked Roman Empire? The only logical explanation is that the church was composed largely of spiritual Christians, men and women filled with and controlled by the Holy Spirit. They knew that before they could experience fellowship with God and be used by Him, to help fulfill His purpose in the world and build His Kingdom, they needed to be filled with His Holy Spirit. And before they could be filled with His Holy Spirit, they needed to be willing to be forgiven and cleansed of their sins.

Moral Detergents

Many people are trying all kinds of moral detergents, but the stains and blotches are all part of their nature. Moral reforms, social adjustments, therapeutic psychology, sensitivity seminars, etc. ... all these have failed to produce a "new person." The only hope for sinful man is a supernatural cleansing, and only Jesus Christ, through His death on the cross, makes it possible for us to be forgiven. This cleansed life can be experienced only by God's power, not by our own will. The living Christ dwelling within us makes all the difference. The psalmist, King David, understood the need for cleansing and forgiveness of sin. Listen to his heartwarming prayer in Psalm 51:1-19.

He prayed the following:

- Wash me thoroughly from my iniquity.
- And cleanse me from my sin.
- For I acknowledge my transgressions.
- And my sin is ever before me.
- Create in me a clean heart, Oh God.
- And renew a right spirit within me.
- Restore unto me the joy of thy salvation.
- And uphold me with thy free spirit.
- Then will I teach transgressors thy ways.
- And sinners shall be converted unto thee.

Cleansing from our sins is a pre-requisite for the abundant and fruitful life to which Christ has called us.

The Great Challenge

Today we live in the most desperate hour of human history. The whole world is in a state of crisis and chaos. No one word so characterizes the mood of our day as does the word *revolution* — revolution in every facet of society and in every country of the world — politically, socially, economically and even religiously. The entire world is filled with fear, anxiety and frustration.

Human solutions without number have been proposed and yet the crisis becomes increasingly worse. Thus, through the process of elimination, men are beginning to turn back to God. The opportunity for presenting the claims of Christ is greater today than at any previous time in recorded history. The Spirit of God has created an unprecedented hunger in the hearts of multitudes of the earth. What an exciting hour to be alive to serve the King of kings and Lord of lords! Both children and adults are turning to Christ in ever-increasing numbers. Even so, this great harvest is being accomplished by relatively few Christians. This is why the Lord wants you to learn and start teaching others. He has told me that time is running out.

The vast majority of Christian's still live defeated and in sterility. The average layman and many pastors seldom, if ever, introduce another person to Christ. What has happened to the Christians of our generation?

The Great Problem

Even today, more than three quarters of our nation's population professes to be Christian. More than 88% of a large cross-section interviewed recently said that they believe in God. Yet our attitudes and actions prove that our nation has become a corrupt and a materialistic nation – morally and spiritually decadent. Many Christians have become more a part of the problems in the society than a part of the solution. Non-Christians see little or no difference in the quality of life between themselves and the average Christian.

An Example

A Christian friend, a pillar of his church once confided, "I used to encourage my neighbor to go with me to church. He always refused, but I persisted. One day he said to me, 'George, do not pester me anymore about going to your church. Obviously it has not done you any good. I see nothing about your life that is any different from mine. We live basically the same kind of lives. In short, I do not want your religion, and I do not want to hear anymore about it." Many young people have left the church because they feel that their parents and other adults are hypocrites, professing something with their lips that they do not demonstrate in their lives.

My Visits to Heaven and Hell

The Wrong Way

(See Matthew 5:43-48 and 7:1-23). I have found, as I have had the privilege of speaking to hundreds of Christians around the nation, that the average defeated, frustrated, fruitless Christian is not happy with his spiritual condition. He would like to change, but he does not know what to do. This kind of person does not need to be rebuked or criticized and condemned; he needs to be loved and helped.

An Example

Some time ago, when I was driving through the city, I made a wrong turn. I found myself driving against traffic on a one-way street. The people on the sidewalk started telling me I was going in the wrong direction. But I had already realized this in the split second after I had turned. My problem was not to determine whether or not I was going the wrong direction; it was how to get turned around. I soon succeeded in changing my direction, through the help of a friendly policeman, and I went on my way rejoicing, driving with the traffic.

So it is in the Christian life. If he is a defeated Christian, one does not need to be told that he is a hypocrite or that his life is not honoring to our Lord; he needs to understand the nature of his problem and how to find a solution to it. This is exactly what the Word of God does for us.

Message No. 5

Faith Is Like a Muscle

What is faith? Faith is another word for trust. Faith must have an object. The Christian's object of faith is God and His Word. His Word tells us that we need not continue to be defeated, carnal, fruitless and impotent Christians. We can be fruitful witnesses for Christ, and that is what He has called us to be.

The Lord Jesus Christ gave incredible, but reliable, promise that if we believe in Him we will be able to do greater works than He did. He assured us that whatsoever we ask in His name He will do it. No Christian needs to continue to be a carnal man.

It is important that we recognize that it is our Lord and Savior, Jesus Christ, the object of our faith, has both the power and the willingness to deliver us from carnality. We do not have faith in faith itself. For example, a person could have great faith that the ice on a pond would be thick enough to support his weight. Through his faith, he may boldly walk out on thin ice and get very wet.

On the other hand, a person who may have very weak faith may move slowly out onto a pond of thick ice. As he walks on the ice and realizes its ability to support his weight, his faith in the ice increases. So it is in the Christian life. We place our faith, even a faith that may be very weak, in a trustworthy God and His Word. The better we know God, the more we can trust Him, and the more we can trust Him, the more we experience the reality of His love, grace and power. Faith is like a muscle; it grows with exercise.

Practical Atheists

A man booked passage on a ship with just enough money to buy a ticket, a block of cheese and some crackers for the long voyage. The first few days at sea the crackers and cheese tasted good, but eventually they became stale. Each day, as he watched the porters and waiters carry large steaks, lobsters, chicken and many other delicious foods to the other guests, he became very hungry.

In fact, he became so hungry that he finally stopped one of the porters. "I'll do anything to get one of those steaks," he said. "I'll wash the dishes, clean rooms, even mop the deck."

The porter replied, "You bought a ticket, didn't you? The meals come with the ticket."

Too many people are ignorant, cheese-and-cracker Christians, missing out on all of God's steak dinners. It is tragically true that the average Christian is a practical atheist. He professes to believe in God, yet he acts as though God either does not exist, or is unwilling to help him. He has all the resources of God available, yet he lives in self-imposed spiritual poverty on a roller coaster of emotions. He fails to act as a child of the

King or live as one who has been adopted into royalty from a state of poverty and illiteracy. How can the carnal man get off this emotional roller-coaster type of existence and overcome his inconsistent way of life?

Personal Appropriation

"Spiritual breathing" is a principle which enables believers to live a consistent Christian life. Just as we exhale and inhale physically, so we can also exhale and inhale spiritually.

Exhale and Inhale

We exhale when we confess our sins, and we inhale when we appropriate the fullness of God's Spirit by faith. The Bible promises, according to 1 John 1:9, is that if we confess our sins, He (God) is faithful and righteous to forgive us our sins and to cleanse us from all unrighteousness.

Confession (*homologeo* in Greek) suggests agreement with God concerning our sins. Such agreement involves at least three considerations. First, I acknowledge that my sin or sins, which should be named specifically, are wrong and, therefore, are grievous to God. Second, I acknowledge that God has already forgiven my sins – past, present and future – because of Christ's death on the cross. It is essential to realize that this means there is nothing I can do that will add anything to what He has already done for me. Third, I repent, which means that I change my attitude toward my sins. Through the enabling power of the Holy Spirit, this will result in a change in my conduct. Instead of doing what my old, sinful nature, my fleshy self, wants to do, I now do what God wants me to do.

God loves us unconditionally, whether we are good or bad. As Jesus Christ illustrates so movingly in the story of the Prodigal Son, the father, at the insistence of his younger son, gave him his share of the family estate. This he soon wasted on parties and prostitutes. Yet, when he returned home in hunger and defeat, professing his unworthiness to be a son, his father ran to meet him, embraced and kissed him, put a ring on his finger and shoes on his feet, and held a banquet in his honor. This is real with exhaling.

Walking in Unity

Let those who have an "ear to hear" realize that when the trumpet alarm is sounding, they must start packing up to move on. Those who do not want to follow the cloud of glory will shout, "You are causing division." But when the cloud moves, when the alarm sounds and we sense that God is moving us on, we must be prepared to move. The most tragic division is when God moves, and His people don't follow and so, become separated from Him and each other. Because they were too comfortable and settled, they failed to move on.

Some even think that the Baptism in the Holy Spirit is the pinnacle of spirituality. This is Feast of Pentecost. But beyond that there is the Feast of Trumpets, the Day of Atonement and the Feast of Tabernacles. Our pursuit of the Lord's presence must ever be in the spirit of "my utmost for God's highest."

The trumpet is calling the Body together to the door of the Tabernacle of the congregation. God says, "There will I meet with you." Let us move on from the Feast of Pentecost into the unity and love of the Feast of Trumpets, then further into God's plans and purposes – together. Let us lay aside our denominational, tribalistic, sectarianism and become one with Christ and all become members of His Body – the true Church.

A Battle Rages

The age into which we have come is one of spiritual warfare directed at mankind. Humanity is destined to be redeemed or damned, and a battle rages for every life, for every family, for every town and for every nation.

The Church of Jesus Christ needs desperately to experience the authority of God, so that we may win the day in our own personal circumstances and also in the wider affairs of men. What each believer desires is that somehow he may be able to speak to his problems with the authority of Jesus Christ. We do not just need authority, but also the profound wisdom of God. We need to understand our circumstances and then receive authority over them.

My Visits to Heaven and Hell

Access to the throne — the presence of God — is what we need. At the mercy of the throne is all the wisdom and authority we need, for there Christ sits enthroned. From the throne, Christ reigns. If we can experience His throne presence in our lives, we will receive authority and wisdom. We need to seek the Lord more (see Psalm 126:5-6, Zephaniah 2:3, Jeremiah 29:13 and Isaiah 44:3 and 55:6).

Message No. 6

Financial Planning God's Way

For the love of money is the root of all evil: which while some coveted after, they have erred from the faith, and pierced themselves through with many sorrows. 1 Timothy 6:10

When it comes to the issue of material prosperity, many Christians adopt divergent or different views. They range from:

- Some take the position that it is sinful to prosper materially and use Bible passages such as the one quoted above or the parable of rich man and Lazarus to support their case.
- Others take the opposite extreme position of amassing wealth (the so-called Prosperity Gospel).
- Yet others are somewhere in between and get confused as a result.

My own position is that the Bible makes it clear that God wants the best for us, as His children. This includes both spiritual as well as material well-being, but we need to understand how this works, according to God's plan. God has promised us blessing (both spiritual and physical), but we have to fulfill certain conditions. Let us look at each issue in turn.

Material prosperity is part of God's promises. God promised a blessing and desires a blessed life for His children. That means us. John 10:10 has the promise that Jesus has come that we may have life and have it more abundantly. I believe that having an abundant life applies both spiritually and materially (see 2 Corinthians 9:6-8 and Deuteronomy 28:1-14). In verse 8 especially, the Lord will command the blessing on your storehouse, on all to which you set your hand, and He will bless you in the land which the Lord your God is giving you. 3 John 2 is also very explicit. It says:

Beloved, I wish above all things that thou mayest prosper and be in health, even as thy soul prospereth.
3 John 2

"All things" and "health" refer to our physical well-being, while the soul prospering refers to our spiritual well-being.

What Do We Need to Do?

In the Bible, we often see God giving us conditions attached to His promises in the Ten Commandments. The commandment regarding obeying and honoring our parents has a promise attached (that it may be well with us and that our days on earth will be long). I have noted three things among many, as conditions that we need to fulfill in order to enjoy our material blessings: 1) We must love God, 2) We must obey Him, and 3) We must do His will!

Loving God

In Matthew 6:33 we are told to seek first the kingdom of God and His righteousness, and all these things shall be added to us. In this passage, Jesus was referring to people's worries about material well-being. He told His disciples (and us), as a result, to first seek God and love Him, and then the material blessings will follow.

Proverbs 8:21 expounds on these conditions further:

That I may cause those that love me to inherit substance; and I will fill their treasures.
Proverbs 8:21

Responsibility Means Decisiveness

Christian leaders who are decisive make decisions according to their moral convictions, and they take responsibility for their decisions. A leader's ability to make decisions is essential for an organization to move ahead and get the appropriate things done at the right time.

Responsible Christian Leaders:

- Keep hope alive in their organization, no matter how difficult things seem.

- Accept responsibility for what is going on in the lives of those who work for them.
- Know the importance of hope and faith in the lives of those around them.
- Look truthfully at the facts.
- Do not worry if something is inconvenient.
- Make decisions and take actions to reach their goals.
- Are problem solvers who do what it takes to prevent problems.
- Do not blame others for their troubles.
- Acknowledge and take responsibility for their choices.
- Are not to be used to meet their own personal needs.

The Responsibilities of an Effective Christian Leader

- A leader must be observant; he/she must learn to see clearly when he/she looks.
- He/she must be attentive to hear correctly when he/she listens.
- He/she must be thoughtful and think carefully when he/she speaks.
- He/she must trust his/her instincts and inquire critically when he/she doubts.
- He/she must have a servant's spirit and show respect to those he/she serves.

- He/she must be a person of integrity who does what is right when he/she acts.
- He/she must foresee and consider the consequence of his/her decisions.
- He/she must be temperate, having his/her emotions under control and remaining calm when he/she is challenged.
- He/she must use his/her authority, power and influence to earn the respect of others and instill faith; he/ she does not manipulate people.
- He/she must be conscientious and careful in his/her commitments.
- Consistence and punctual, a mature leader will be able to display a depth of understanding.
- He/she musts be able to distinguish between appearances and reality.
- He/she must be alert and broad-minded.
- He/she must sustain a high level of concentration, giving undivided attention to most important issues.
- He/she must think before taking action, especially where other people are concerned.
- He/she must use common sense.
- He/she must demonstrate innovative insight by thinking futuristically.
- He/she must demonstrate intellectual inquisitiveness.
- He/she must demonstrate a positive mental outlook.

Confidence

In Proverbs 3:5 we are told to trust in the Lord with all our heart. Unfortunately, the reality of our flesh is that it is very difficult to totally trust God with all of our heart in every situation. Failure, either ours or someone else's, weighs heavily on our thinking, when we are in a position to trust God in an area we have never had to before. It is human nature to be very cautious, even to the point of not following God at all. The reason is very simple. Experience is a powerful good or bad teacher (see Matthew 21:21-22). We thank God for His mercy because the fact is that most Christians live in doubt all the time.

Doubt is the product of not trusting God. If we do not trust God, then God cannot fulfill His promises to us in the area we fail to trust Him. James tells us not to be double-minded, for a double-minded man will not receive anything from God. This is a hard teaching to receive because most of us live right here.

So how does a person overcome doubt regarding the things of God? In Proverbs 3:5 we are taught to lean not on our own understanding. We need to learn to lean on God's understanding of our circumstances. When we are weak, He is strong (see 2 Corinthians 12:10). You have to position yourself to win, first, in your spirit (there should be no doubt at all that Jesus Christ is Lord of your heart), second, in your mind (He has to be sovereign Lord over your whole thought process, understand that you are better than all the circumstances set before you). Then, in your physical being, you must take the actions of a champion. Action does not mean lip service, hypocrisy or false piety. It means taking steps. In our Christian walk, God is constantly reinforcing through the Word how great we really are. He expects us to win every time:

We are more than conquerors through him that loved us. Romans 8:37

Thanks be to God, which giveth us the victory through our Lord Jesus Christ.
1 Corinthians 15:57

Message No. 7

Confession and Forgiveness

If you are a Christian, your sins (past, present and future) have been forgiven. Pleadings, tears, personal efforts and religious rituals cannot provide reconciliation with God. They are not needed. Faith is simply believing and claiming as truth what Jesus Christ has said and what He has already done for us. Faith enables us to view ourselves as God views us: as His children, loved, forgiven and cleansed.

Faith motivates us to repent. Repentance, which is derived from Greek, means "a change of mind," resulting, through the enabling of the Holy Spirit, in a change of action. It will cause us to turn from what we have been doing which displeased God to doing what God wants us to do.

In Hebrews 10, we discovered that what man tried to do concerning his sins was in vain, but Christ did it for him through His death on the cross and by shedding His blood. We cannot add anything to what Christ has already done. We simply accept His forgiveness and cleansing by faith. It may be that there is sin or disobedience in our hearts, but confession brings hidden destroyers into the open.

There can never be healing of sinner's problems until they have confessed sin, and renounced and forsaken it. Be open and honest before God. He is a loving Father who wants to heal you and not a dreadful monster who wishes to punish you. He does not want to uncover these problem areas to embarrass or shame you. He wants to get them out of your heart and mind, because they are poisoning and destroying you. If God makes you aware of some sin or resentment, which is out of harmony with His will, confess it to Him (see Galatians 4:5-6).

Why confess?

You may wonder why, as a Christian, you need to confess, if Christ has already paid the penalty for your sin. It should be understood that confession does not result in forgiveness, since Christ has forgiven us once and for all, according to Hebrews 10. Confession is necessary only as an expression of faith and as an act of obedience to claim God's promise. Confession makes real in your own experience what God has done for you through the death of His Son. The benefits are not simply psychological, but are real and valid, based upon the Word of God.

If you refuse to be honest with God in confessing your sins, you become carnal and walk in the shadows, instead of walking in God's light. The Bible says that if we are living in the light of God's presence, just as Christ does, then we have wonderful fellowship and joy with each other, and the blood of Jesus Christ, His Son, cleanses us from every sin. Perhaps you have committed sins, and have not experienced God's forgiveness. You may feel some resentment toward friends or members of your family. You may have lost the joy of your relationship with Christ. You pray, but there is no response. You read the Bible but get little joy or help from it. You witness for Christ, but no one responds. Join me as we bow our heads together in prayer:

> *Lord Jesus, I trust that after each one has soberly evaluated and inventoried his life, he'll be able to say with the apostle Paul, "I am what I am by the grace of God." Lord, I pray that we will be inspired to go out and work more diligently and fully pour out our lives to cause Your Kingdom to come, Your will to be done on earth, as it is in Heaven. Lord, deliver us from high-mindedness and human ambition and initiative not in line with Your lordship. May understanding of Your purpose for our lives be revealed to us by Your Spirit.*
>
> *Father, help us, we pray, to more fully and effectively serve You in these days of glorious opportunity. We give You praise and thanksgiving, as we ask this all in the matchless name of Jesus. Amen!*

Short-Circuiting God's Power

One day I was operating the controls of my daughter's electric train, and the train suddenly stopped running. I could not figure out what was wrong. I took the train apart and put it back together. I pushed the plug in and out of the socket. But nothing happened. Then I discovered that a little piece of metal, which had fallen across the track, was causing the problem. Just a tiny piece of metal, a "no left-turn" had fallen across the negative and positive rails of the train, so the train would no longer move.

In like manner, sin short-circuits the power of God. God is holy and will have nothing to do with sin. But God loves us, even though we may have unconfessed sin/s in our lives. He has forgiven us. All that we need to do to experience afresh the wonder of His love and the joy of His promises is to confess our sins, exalt Him spiritually and experience the reality of His cleansing power.

Message No. 8

God Wants His Word to Work So We Need to Find the Kind of Faith That "Speaks" and Things Happen

A Mustard Seed — God Speaks

Some years ago, I discovered that Weymouth's translation says in Mark 17:20, *"If you had faith that grows as a grain of mustard seed ... ."* When I read that, the Spirit caused me to understand Jesus' teaching in a new way. It was a way I had never heard anyone explain faith before.

Jesus was not telling us that all we need is a tiny bit of faith, like a tiny mustard seed, and then we can move trees and mountains. Rather, the Lord was teaching us that faith that grows as a grain of mustard seed can heal the sick, cast out demons and see signs following.

Paul recognized that it took all, total or full-grown faith to move mountains. You do not move mountains with seed faith; you move mountains with total faith. It takes a fully-developed faith to relocate a mountain. Paul recognized this and Jesus also taught it in Matthew 17.

During this time, there came to the other nine apostles waiting below, a certain man who had a son who was lunatic. This caused him to fall into fire and into water. The nine apostles tried exorcism, but with no success. Then the man came to Jesus, upon His descent from the mountain, and said, *"I brought him [my son] to thy disciples, and they could not cure him"* (Matthew 17:16).

Faith starts with God giving to everyone of us the measure of seed faith. The word *measure* comes from the Greek word *metron,* meaning "a limited portion." This seed (a limited portion or measure) is God's gift to every believer.

There is no Christian who can say, "I don't have faith," because the Scriptures say that God deals to every man the measure, or seed, of faith. Further support for this is found in Ephesians 2:8-9. In 1 Corinthians 13:2, Paul comments on faith that moves mountains:

> *And though I have the gift of prophecy and understand all mysteries and all knowledge; and though I have all faith, so that I could remove mountains, and have not charity, I am nothing.*   1 Corinthians 13:2

There are two kinds of faith: the gift of faith and developed faith. We need to distinguish between the two:

The Gift of Faith

This is the gift of faith mentioned in 1 Corinthians 12:9. It is a sovereign impartation, or gift, of faith from God to you.

Developed Faith

This is the developed faith in you. With developed faith, if you start with 5% faith and it grows to 75% faith, then you can deal with any situation that you encounter up to 75% faith. On the other hand, if your faith has not progressively grown, but you have only known a sudden gift or impartation of faith on some singular occasion, your faith development might still be at the 5% level.

We must now discover how faith can grow in the life of the believer. We go (or grow) "from faith to faith" and from glory to glory." A scriptural truth to remember is this: you will know the glory of God in your life only in proportion to the development of faith in your life. Developed faith will bring an increase of God's glory resting on your life and ministry.

The principle of growing faith can be illustrated in a story of King Tut's tomb (Tut being a common abbreviation for Tutankhamun). He was a famous Egyptian pharaoh, buried about 1357 B.C. in an extremely elaborate pyramid. His tomb was discovered completely intact in 1922 by an English archeologist. Inside, among other treasures, was found honey, wheat and corn.

The natural law of growth teaches us spiritual things. A grain of wheat in the wrong environment will never grow. However, given the right conditions, it will not only grow; but, through the replanting of each successive harvest, it will eventually produce thousands of bushels of wheat.

This same tremendous potential is locked up in the seed of faith which God has dealt to every man. What we do with it determines whether it grows or remains a seed. In order to grow, the seed must have nourishment – fertile soil, water and sunshine. Metaphorically, the seed of faith, in order to grow, must be nurtured in the soil of God's Word (not the letter, but the Living Word revealed by the Spirit of revelation, see Ephesians 1:17).

When we speak of God's Word as being the soil in which the seed of faith grows, we are not referring only or solely to the Holy Bible. Romans 10:17 says that faith cometh by hearing the word of God. This use of *word* is from the Greek *rhema*, meaning a living word.

First of all, we must understand what it means to hear. In Romans 10:17, Paul is not talking about the passive act of listening to a sermon preached from the Bible. He is not suggesting that we go to church five times a week in order for faith to grow. Faith comes, grows and is demonstrated and expressed by hearing and then acting upon what we have heard (see Romans 10:17 and James 1:22: *"But be ye doers of the word, and not hearers only, deceiving your own selves."*)

Too often, when God speaks to us, we go right on with whatever we are doing, and do not take any action as a result of what God has just said to us. And then we wonder why we do not have a growth in faith. Faith has not been released and cannot grow until it has been acted upon. Each time you hear and act, you take another step of faith.

You do not cast out a legion of devils until you have cast out one. That is to say, you do not reach out to do something beyond your faith development, trying to go from seed faith to full-grown faith in one big leap. It does not work that way. Faith grows by a series of progressive steps (see Galatians 2:1). Here Paul is talking about fourteen years later.

A word of caution here: never try to act on God's Word to somebody else. You cannot imitate another man's faith. Some have tried to imitate great healing ministries, with hapless and often tragic results. Others have tried to follow someone else's step of faith, and have tripped and fallen flat. Another of the basic essentials for the growth of faith is love (see Galatians 5:6).

In John 14:21, Jesus deals with the relationship of love to obedience. In verses 23-24, we hear His Word to us, and because we love Him, we act on what we have heard. If we do not obey, we do not love, and then faith does not work. Without the exercise of faith, there is no growth of faith. Faith, therefore, grows by obedience, which flows out of our love for Jesus, in response to hearing the Word of the Lord.

When the Scriptures say, *"Faith cometh by hearing ... the word of God,"* this refers to the subjective experience by which God speaks to us, an actual verse in the Bible or the same way He spoke to the prophets of old.

He Does Speak

The prophets either heard audibly, inwardly by dream, by vision, by angelic visitation or through the mouth of one communicated with. This communication is what the Bible calls 'the Word of God.'

There is the enscriptured (or written) Word of God and the living Word of the Lord. We need to know the distinction between them, in order to further understand what is meant by hearing the Word of the Lord.

God still speaks today by the Holy Spirit, through His written Word, through His anointed servants and through such supernatural means as dreams, visions, inward assurances and the divine providence of circumstance.

God never speaks to us in any subjective experience in contradiction to His written Word. All such experience must be judged by and agree with the Holy Scriptures. We need to open our hearts to receive the Word of the Lord, not only from the Bible, but also through the other channels by which God speaks.

The seven-times-repeated warning in Revelation 2:7 is for us to heed in this day: *"He that hath an ear, let him hear what the Spirit saith unto the churches."* Note the use of the present continuous tense, *"saith,"* meaning "to hear what the Spirit says and continues to say."

This same tense is used by Jesus in Matthew 4:4: *"Man shall not live by bread alone, but by every word that proceedeth [present continuous tense] out of the mouth of God."* We live not only by what God said, but also by what He is presently sayings, what proceeds and continues to proceed out of the mouth of God.

We walk in life by hearing and obeying the proceeding Word of the Lord, by whatever means He chooses to speak that Word to us. When we refuse to accept that God can speak to us through other means than the written pages of the Bible, we may cut ourselves off from communication with Him, and spiritual death begins to set in.

Safe faith is based on hearing, obedience and love. We open our spirit to the voice of the Lord by having an open responsive heart, to hear and to obey, because we love Him, and He loves us. It is because of that love that faith works. Otherwise, faith is stifled and ceases to grow. Hearing, obeying and loving then, are the three central ingredients to the growth of faith.

- In Mark 11:22-23, there is a higher faith than "asking" faith. It takes faith to ask, but there is a faith that goes beyond asking, to a faith that speaks.
- The progression and growth of faith is related to what you say or speak forth with the very words of your mouth (see Proverbs 4:20-22). We have what we say. The moment that we face a

situation, the response in our heart is expressed by our mouth, and we speak what we believe. Jesus admonished this in Matthew 12:34-37.

- God promised to make Abraham the father of many nations. Although Abraham was close to a hundred years old and beyond bringing forth a progeny, he was not weak in faith. Nor did his faith falter at the deadness of Sarah's womb. This means that he went about positively praising God for all the things that He had promised him, confessing what God had said and giving Him the glory. Abraham had heard God's Word, and was fully persuaded that what He had promised He was able also to perform. One of the reasons the Lord appoints teachers is to enable them to deal with unbelief.

Elizabeth Saidimu

Message No. 9

Praying in the Spirit

Power in prayer is only for those humble enough to acknowledge that they do not know how to pray. The Holy Spirit is looking for people like that, so He can empower them in prayer. *"Likewise the Spirit also helpeth our infirmities: for we know not what we should pray for as we ought: but the Spirit itself maketh intercession for us with groanings which cannot be uttered"* (Romans 8:26). Only if we have the Holy Spirit's enablement in prayer can we obey the command given by Paul in Ephesians 6:18: *"Praying always with all prayer and supplication in the Spirit, and watching thereunto with all perseverance and supplication for all saints."*

What is prayer in the Spirit? And how is it different from other forms or modes of prayer?

Different Forms of Prayer

There are many ways we can approach the Lord in prayer. All are important and have their place in the church and in our walk with God.

1. Contemplative or Meditative Prayer

Some religious orders have given their whole life to prayer. They are devoted to knowing God and relating to His will through meditation, quiet thought and prayer. Their concern for the world is basically brought forth through intercessory prayer on behalf of others. This is a noble and important form of prayer. However, those involved in this kind of praying seldom learn to pray in the Spirit.

2.   The Use of Prayer Books

Many read their prayers out of prayer books. We have a prayer book in the Bible called the book of Psalms. When such prayers are read with a heart that is truly seeking after God, the Holy Spirit can bring the life of the living Word to their written words.

3.   Directed Prayers

Others repeat directed prayers. Many of us have had someone help or direct us in our first prayer. Little children are taught to pray by their parents. We often lead people in saying the sinner's prayer.

I recently witnessed a heartwarming and humorous event related to directed prayer. In a church, at the end of the service, a young man asked a visitor if he wanted to receive Christ as Savior. "No, I don't believe I'm ready yet," was the visitor's reply.

The young man then asked, "Would you know what to pray when you are ready?"

"No, I guess I wouldn't," was the visitor's honest response.

"Would you like to know?" was the next question. The answer was, "Yes, I believe I would."

The young man then said, "Here is the prayer you should pray. Just repeat it after me," and he led the visitor in a simple directed prayer of repentance. He was telling the visitor what to pray to invite Jesus to come into his heart and be his Lord and Savior. As the visitor repeated that prayer, tears began trickling from his eyes. Then his face lit up with joy. The Holy Spirit had melted his resistance, and Christ came into his heart, and he was truly born again.

Yes, God honors all kinds of prayer, if we are sincere and ask in faith. However, as wonderful as this may be, it is not praying in the Spirit.

4. Shopping-List Prayers

Another form of prayer is what some call "the shopping-list" approach. Some of us have a list of needs and desires which we bring to God in prayer. We write them down so we do not forget to keep on praying until we receive God's answer. The list may include request for families, friends, church and leaders. When our motives are right, this, too, is a form of prayer that results in blessing.

In fact, James 4:2 tells us: *"We have not because we ask not."* An example of this is the story of the Prodigal Son (see Luke 15:11-31). The younger brother had asked for and received his inheritance (his part of the family fortune). In rebellion, he then left his father and elder brother and went away to live a sinful life. Many months later, he repented and returned home. His inheritance now gone, he was homeless and in poverty. His father joyfully welcomed him home, forgave him and called for a feast to celebrate the return of his prodigal son.

The elder brother complained to his father, "You never blessed me with a feast" (see verses 29-30). The father simply replied, *"Son, thou art ever with me, and all that I have is thine"* (Verse 31). He could have had a feast anytime he desired. But the elder brother did not ask, so he did not receive. It seems that he was living far below his privilege. If he had wanted more, all he had to do was ask. This was his right, as a first born son.

The Abuse of Prayer and Spiritual Gifts

There are two mistakes we can make in relationship to prayer. The first is failing to ask. The second is more serious: asking selfishly for what *we* want, even if what we're asking is contrary to what God wants. James talks about these problems: *"Ye lust, and have not: ye kill, and desire to have, and cannot obtain: ye fight and war, yet ye have not, because ye ask not. Ye ask, and receive not, because ye ask amiss, that ye may consume it upon your lusts."* (James 4:2-3). Let us take a closer look at these three failures:

1. Praying Out of Lust

This word *lust* is a very forceful word in the Greek language in which the New Testament was written.

Elizabeth Saidimu

It speaks of any excessive desire on the part of man, usually evil in nature. Paul refers to this in his letters of advice and counsel to Timothy:

- *"Foolish and hurtful lusts"* (1 Timothy 6:9)
- *"Flee ... youthful lusts"* (2 Timothy 2:22).
- *"Led away with divers lusts"* (2 Timothy 3:6)

Lust is wanting something very badly. It is related to greed or selfish desire and covetousness, which is wanting what someone else has. It expresses itself in many ways. There is the lust for a prominent position, power, money and immoral pleasures.

If we use prayers to serve our lusts, we put ourselves in spiritual danger. We will miss out on God because our motives are wrong. We are actually praying from a greedy or lustful spirit.

Some have been taught that prayer is a means of getting anything we want from God. If you have been taught that way, you may not even realize you are praying amiss. Prayer is not to acquire all the material things we can dream of. Our prayers should primarily be to discover what God desires. Our energies and prayers should be focused on seeking first the kingdom of God and His righteousness. Then, Jesus promised, all of the things we need in this life will be added to us (see Matthew 6:33).

God knows what things we need and promises to provide them — if we seek the Kingdom of God and His righteousness first. If we seek material things rather than God's Kingdom, we can move in a direction displeasing to God and spiritually dangerous for ourselves.

2. Praying Amiss

One of the greatest judgments God can send upon us is to give us exactly what we wrongfully insist He give us in prayer. If our prayer arises from a wrong motive, He may withhold the answer for a time. But if we keep asking wrongfully, He may give us what we want, but with that answer will come judgment

> *And he gave them their request; but sent leanness into their soul.* Psalm 106:15

The children of Israel grew tired of their daily diet of manna, so they asked God for flesh to eat. *"But [they] lusted exceedingly in the wilderness, and tempted God in the desert"* (Psalm 106:14). The Lord finally gave them what they had asked for, but He also sent disease and death to their bodies. Praying wrongfully can indeed bring a very sad outcome to our lives.

3. Praying with Wrong Motives and Attitudes

We can abuse or misuse the gifts of God. The story of the prophet Balaam is a good example of the abuse of a spiritual gift (see Numbers 22:24). Balaam had a true gift of prophecy. His prophecies are the most eloquent in the whole Bible. None of his prophecies failed. The problem with Balaam was not his gift or his ministry; it was his motives. He used his gift to gain fame and fortune for himself.

He was promised gold and glory, if he would prophesy for King Balak and curse the people of God. Balaam asked God if he should go to King Balak:

And God said unto Balaam, thou shalt not go with them, and thou shalt not curse the people.
Numbers 22:12

At first Balaam obeyed, but he kept asking God for permission to go. Finally, God let Balaam have his way, but He placed an angel with a drawn sword in the path to kill Balaam. Balaam was unable to see the angel, although the donkey on which he rode could clearly see it. Balaam's lust for fame and fortune had blinded his prophetic vision. Only his faithful donkey saved his life that day.

The Bible tells us the reasons God deceives disobedient servants:

And for this cause God shall send them strong delusion, that they should believe a lie: that they all might be damned who believed not the truth, but had pleasure in unrighteousness.
2 Thessalonians 2:11-12

Balaam's motives and attitudes were wrong. He was willing to curse God's people for his own fame and fortune. He took *"pleasure in unrighteousness,"* therefore God sent him a strong delusion. He was so blinded by his unrighteous motive and actions that he could not even see the sword the angel was ready to use to kill him. The final outcome of the story was sad and tragic, for both Balaam and Israel. Balaam died for his sin (see Numbers 31:8 and Luke 22:42).

The Holy Spirit Helps Us to Pray

Paul calls on us and encourages us to pray in Spirit. As we shall see, this is one sure way to avoid praying "amiss." Paul develops this very thought in Romans. He carefully explains to us how the Holy Spirit can help us, as we yield to Him when we pray.

We do not even know how or what to pray for as we should. The Holy Spirit, however, helps us in our weakness. He does this by praying for us and through us with sounds and sighs too deep to put into words. God knows our hearts and the mind of the Spirit, and the Holy Spirit always prays for the saints according to or in line with God's will (see Romans 8.26-27).

Church leaders constantly face circumstances and problems that they really do not know how or what to pray for. Sometime problems can be so great and people's lives so mixed up, that we are not sure how to help them. There are many different kinds of problems, and they can involve decisions regarding: people, places, finances, health and spiritual needs.

Often, it seems, people's lives are like a fishnet that has become all tangled up in one big bundle. We do not know where to begin trying to untangle it. We want to do the right thing in the right way, with the right people, in the right place, and for the right reasons, but where do we start?

What a comfort it is to realize that the Holy Spirit knows us better than we know ourselves. He knows who we are, where we are, and how we are. He also knows the Father's will and answer for every need. His wisdom and power make up for our lack of knowledge. The Holy Spirit compensates for our weakness and deficiencies in prayer. And, more than that, He is ready to put the words we pray in our mouth, so that we pray according to Gods' will. How does this happen? It happens when we pray in the Spirit.

Praying in the Spirit

This phrase, *praying in the Spirit*, is used in the New Testament to describe a kind of praying that by-passes the limitation of our intellect and knowledge. In Jude 20, we are encouraged to build up ourselves on our most holy faith, praying in the Holy Ghost. In Ephesians 6:18, Paul tells us to enter the war against principalities and powers by praying always with prayer of supplication in the Spirit.

The Gift of Tongues as Given for Prayer

In 1 Corinthians 14:14, Paul writes: *"If I pray in a tongue, my spirit prayeth."* One of the primary uses of the gift of tongues is to pray in the Spirit. As it is written:

> For he that speaketh in an unknown tongue speaketh not unto men, but unto God. 1 Corinthians 14:2

Using the gift of tongues in prayer is one of the blessed side benefits of being baptized in the Holy Spirit.

The Holy Spirit Enables Us

When we yield to the Holy Spirit's action upon us, we begin praying in the Spirit. Paul teaches us that three important things take place when we pray in the Spirit (see Romans 8:26-27): 1) The Holy Spirit enables us to pray God's prayers, 2) The Holy Spirit enables us to feel God's feelings, and 3) The Holy Spirit enables us to think God's thoughts.

We must yield to the Spirit

Some years ago we were conducting a day of fasting and prayer, and an elderly prophetess by the name of Ruth was part of the prayer team I was leading. To my amazement, when Ruth laid hands on someone's head and started praying, she seemed to know all about them. She mentioned intimate details of their life that no one but the person she was praying for knew. As she prayed, the person for whom she was praying would break into sobs of appreciation and thanks to the Lord because they knew Ruth's prayers were borne from Heaven. They knew she was praying in the Holy Spirit, and that she was praying God's prayer. These persons were very encouraged to realize that God knew all about their problems. He loved them enough to cause one of His handmaidens to pray for the most desperate needs of their lives.

> *And thus are the secrets of his heart made manifest; and so falling down on his face he will worship God, and report that God is in you of a truth.*
> 1 Corinthians 14:25

I asked the Lord that very day, "Dear Lord, let me pray like Ruth prays." I am happy to report that in the years since, the Lord has answered that prayer. I have learned to yield to the Spirit's action on my life. He will do the same for you, if you spend daily time in His presence, waiting on Him. You can pray God's prayers, as you learn to use the gifts of tongues, interpretation and prophecy in prayer.

Feeling God's Feelings

In Romans 8:26, Paul tells us that the Holy Spirit makes intercession through us with groanings. The

Spirit's action upon us in prayer can bring an agony of Spirit that is like the labor pains women experience when giving birth to a baby. The Spirit causes us to pray with deep sighs and sounds we cannot put into words. It is God's heart.

The Scriptures tell us there were times when Jesus prayed to the Father in this same way:

> *Who in the days of his flesh, when he had offered up prayers and supplications with strong crying and tears.* Hebrews 5:7

If we yield to the Spirit's action in prayer, we will feel God's feelings. And, oh, what a difference that can make! We will no longer judge people so harshly because we will understand God's love and feeling for them. Then we can help them because love never fails. It always wins.

Thinking God's Thoughts

The Holy Spirit makes intercession through us and for us according to the will of God because He knows the mind of God (see Romans 8:27).

We can avoid praying wrongfully by praying in the Spirit. In doing so, we will pray according to the will of God. Our ministry to others will be a blessing because it will reveal God's will.

This is one important purpose for praying in the Spirit. God often reveals His will through prayer, as we minister to others. I want to share some examples with you.

During a co-workers' meeting, with teams of five or six spiritually-mature saints, we set aside a day for fasting and prayer. That day is spent praying for people who have needs. They come to the prayer team as husband and wife if married and one by one if they are not. Often, God will reveal details about those we are praying for. This is what I mean by the words "thinking God's thoughts." The insights given by the Spirit enable us to help these people repent and quit doing things which may be contributing to their problems. We also receive insights from the Lord so that we can pray for them in specific ways.

The whole prayer team keeps their hearts and minds yielded to the Holy Spirit for His thoughts and direction, and each member may receive some part of God's will for the person who has come for prayer. As revelation comes in this way by God's Spirit, the team member share the thoughts they believe are coming from the Holy Spirit. In this way, others can check or verify the authenticity of what is being shared.

We are not infallible, and we make mistakes when moving in the gifts or enabling of the Holy Spirit, and there is wisdom and safety in having a word from the Lord confirmed or agreed upon by others. When everyone on the team is of the same mind about something, we can have the assurance that we have the true mind of the Lord and then we can follow through on that revelation in prayer. As it is written:

> *In the mouth of two or three witnesses shall every word be established.*   2 Corinthians 13:1

> *Let the prophets speak two or three, and let the other judge.*   1 Corinthians 14:29

In this way, God's will and Word unfolds, as the team waits upon the Lord and each other for the Spirit's thoughts.

Three Examples

1. A Spirit of Infirmity

An example of how the Holy Spirit helps us in our prayers took place at that same meeting. A lady came for prayer for a physical problem, but she herself had a powerful ministry of intercession, praying against the devil and his forces on behalf of others. This is the spiritual warfare we talked about earlier in the book. As we prayed for her, God showed us that her physical problem had a spiritual cause. When she had been praying against the powers of darkness, she was wounded by the enemy, with a blow that affected her physical body. An evil power was the cause, rather than just a natural physical cause. She had not known this and had sought help from doctors.

We faced the devil and his evil forces through the power of prayer and the authority of God's Word, as we prayed in tongues for her. There was a very militant tone that accompanied our prayers. We knew we were battling a spirit of infirmity that was binding her. We commanded her to be released in the strength of the name of Jesus, and she was set free at once.

In this way, through prayer in the Holy Spirit, God's thoughts, insights, mind and will were revealed to us. He caused us to pray God's prayer, to feel God's feeling, and to think God's thoughts.

2. Released to the Lord

Toward the end of the day we were praying with another lady who had a very serious problem. She had a husband and three children in their teen years, and they required a lot of her time and attention. But, in addition to all of her other household chores, she had brought her father to her home to care for him. Because of his advanced age, he was like a baby who needed to wear diapers to catch his bodily waste. He was too weak to sit, stand or walk, so she had to care for him twenty-four hours a day. For lack of sleep and rest, she was on the verge of total physical and emotional collapse. What was she to do?

The Bible says, *"Honour thy father and thy mother, as the LORD thy God hath commanded thee; that thy days may be prolonged, and that it may go well with thee"* (Deuteronomy 5:16). This woman wanted to obey the Bible, but trying to honor her father was leading her to the brink of self-destruction.

I said, "Let us pray in tongues for a few minutes and see if the Holy Spirit responds to our prayer." As the team prayed, the Lord impressed me with something. He made me think God's thoughts. I felt the Spirit reveal the following:

The Lord had come to take this lady's father to Heaven, but while he was dying, she had gotten down besides his bed and rebuked death and commanded in prayer that he live. The Lord said to me, "Because she has taken responsibility for her father, I respect her governance over his life. When she rebuked death and commanded that her father live, I withdrew and left him alive."

I was surprised and shocked by this revelation, and knew that I had to share it with her and ask her if it had really happened. This would verify whether these thoughts were my own or from the Spirit. She confirmed that her father had been near death several times, and she had prayed as I described. We were able to gently counsel her, as we followed her home. We advised her to talk this over with her husband and children and decide if they were all in agreement to release her father to the Lord. He would be happier in Heaven, released from his near-dead, ninety–six-year-old body. This, we advised her, would save her from a nervous breakdown.

The woman did as we advised. She and her family prayed this prayer, and a few nights later, the

Lord came to take her father to Heaven. I'm sure she was sad to lose him, but her problem was solved. I would never have thought of these things in a thousand years, but the Holy Spirit had a simple word of knowledge and word of wisdom for us to give this lady, when we had prayed in other tongues.

3. A Failing Business

In another case, a man wanted me to pray for him that God would save his failing business and cause him to prosper financially. I responded, "I will pray in the Spirit, and then I will ask the Lord to respond to this prayer by causing me to think His thoughts and feel His feelings."

After praying in tongues, I prayed for an interpretation. The man was angry with me for taking so long, but God answered my prayer. As the Holy Spirit prayed through my lips, it brought the man to repentance. Several years later he came back to thank me. He was now blessed and prospered because he had obeyed the Lord.

With every prayer it is our responsibility to do His will here on earth as it is in Heaven. Let us pray at all times and in all ways for God's people everywhere. You will never walk in victory until you know your enemy is defeated.

As Christians, we do not move from defeat into victory. We do not move from doubt into faith. The Scriptures tell us, however, that there is a way of faith

My Visits to Heaven and Hell

which leads to greater faith. It is *"from faith to faith"* (Romans 1:17). Likewise, our starting point for victory is not defeat but victory itself – Christ's victory:

> *But thanks be to God who giveth us the victory through our Lord Jesus Christ.*
> 1 Corinthians 15:57

We must begin in victory, if we are going to have victory. Doubt, defeat and despair are not the kinds of stuff from which we can build a strong victorious life. We can never be winners, as long as we see ourselves as helpless, hopeless and victims of the devil.

Satan no longer has power or authority to defeat the sons and daughters of God's royal family. However, he does have the ability to deceive the children of God — if they do not understand who they are in Christ Jesus.

When I was a younger Christian, I developed a real fear for anything which was satanic or demonic. I do not know how or when such fear began. I was always interested in preachers and what they were doing. Perhaps some of their stories of demonic powers may have sown a seed of fear in my mind without my realization. Later on, I learned that many other Christians have the same problem. After I got saved and filled with the Holy Spirit and as I grew in the Lord, I developed a real desire to have authority over demonic powers. I told the Lord that if I ever came across a demon, I wanted to be able to cast him out. I worried so much about demons having greater power that I would even dream about such an encounter or meeting. In my dream, I would see myself trying to cast out a devil but being unable to do so. It was a very serious point of fear for me at the time. However the heavenly Father saw my desire to be strong and faithful in the family of God, and He met my need and solved my problems in an unexpected way.

I would have thought He might have used mighty angels or great lighting bolts to meet my needs for power and authority over demon forces today, but it did not come in that manner. God had a better way, which I now want to share with you.

God chose to meet my need for power over demonic forces by way of revelation. In a revelation, God shows or reveals to us a truth from scripture which we have not seen or known before. Such truth is always centered in Jesus Christ, and it has the power to set us free from our fears.

Ye shall know the truth, and the truth shall make you free. John 8:32

If the Son therefore shall make you free, ye shall be free indeed. John 8:36

I have found that a revelation which sets me free can be given to others. The truth will work in their lives, just as well as it has in mine. Therefore allow the Holy Spirit to open your heart to God's Word, and God's Word to your heart.

Free from Fear of Death and the Devil

The children of a family share physical features. Jesus, as our Redeemer, took upon Himself our human nature. He did this that He might die. By dying, He gained access to the realm of death so that He could destroy the one who had the power of death — the devil. Jesus did this to release that fear, so now we are free (see Hebrews 2:14-15).

The Devil Is Destroyed

Jesus died that the devil might be destroyed. This is a strong, sure statement, which is absolutely and totally true. It rests upon the full authority of scripture.

When we say that he has been destroyed, that does not mean that he no longer exists. He is still around. *Destroy* means "to make powerless, bring to naught, reduce to zero, make inactive, make of no effect, and paralyze." Through His death, Jesus not only paid the penalty for our sins; He made the devil powerless, reduced him to zero and paralyzed him. Therefore we no longer need to fear the devil or the judgment which follows death (see Hebrews 9:27 and 10:27).

Death Lost Its Sting

Through His death, Jesus also showed us that we need not fear the physical effects of death. Death cannot destroy the soul or spirit of man. After we have died, we will even have a glorified body, like the Lord Himself. This will occur when Christ returns in resurrection power (see 1 Corinthians 15:55).

Christ reigns

The death and resurrection of Jesus has released us from the fear of the devil and death. The devil himself was stripped of his earthly authority. His right to rule over creation was taken away by the crucified Christ. The scepter, or royal symbol of authority, was stripped from his hand. After defeating the devil, Jesus took His rightful place upon the throne.

There is a war which rages within me and which causes me more trouble than any conflict I face. My number one problem is not the devil and his demons, but, rather, myself. Yes, my own sinful nature is my greatest enemy.

As we have seen, we have both eternal and external (inside and outside) enemies. Our outside enemy is the devil and his demons. We have studied principles by which these foes can be overcome. The purpose of this is to deal with our inside enemies. For years I blamed everything on the devil and his demons, and then I learned that most of my spiritual battles were within me. I did not have to look far to find my greatest foe. I found that I face him every morning in the mirror. I also discovered that I am not the only one who faces this problems. This is true of every Christian.

My Visits to Heaven and Hell

A problem this great and this widespread needs a strong solution, and God has the answer. He knows us better than we know ourselves and has provided a remedy for us in Christ Jesus. Accepting this remedy provides us with sure and certain victory.

Our Two Natures

There is a mental disorder which is called Schizophrenia, which means a dual mind. It refers to mental problems in which a person may display symptoms of a dual personality. They will think and act like two different people at one time. They may speak and respond in a normal way, but at another times their behavior will be just the opposite.

There is a kind of spiritual schizophrenia for the Christian. We suffer from what sometimes seems to be a dual personality within. At one time we display in our lives the lovely qualities of Christ's life. We are joyful, peaceful, kind and gracious. At other times, to our dismay, we may be sharp-spoken, short-tempered and hard to live with. We do not want to be this way, but we are.

Even though we try to be sweet, nice and wonderful, we end up being sour, mean and miserable. We know it, and others do too. It seems that we are being pulled in two different directions at once. We feel as if there is a great war being waged within, and we are often on the losing side.

"What is going on?" we may ask ourselves. "Do I have a dual personality?" The answer is simple: yes, you do. When you received Christ into your life, you received a new nature. His nature came into your life as the Spirit of Christ. He took up His home in your heart. The Bible shows that this new state causes a conflict. The old man — our flesh — and the new man — the spirit — are opposites by nature. They are living in the same house, but they have very different desires. The old man is very self-centered, while the new man is very Christ-centered. These two natures are at war with one another. This is the cause of our problem.

God saw that this conflict would arise within us after we accepted His Son as our Lord and Savior, and therefore He has provided a powerful remedy for the problem. His answer centers in the life and death of His Son. It involves a truth which, when understood and acted upon, will give us victory over our enemy within.

Message No. 10

Turning Your Challenge into Blessings

Turning Impossibilities into Possibilities

The world is full of educated derelicts. Anytime the enemy plans evil, God plans good, to counter the evil .Be of good courage, and He shall strengthen your heart, all you that hope in the Lord. Furthermore, I reckon that the sufferings of this present time are not worthy to be compared with the glory which shall be revealed to us. When someone criticizes you and says that it cannot be done, it means that they do not know how to do it themselves. If you listen to negative critics, you will find it difficult to succeed. Life offers enormous blessing for those who persist. Blessings start with accepting life as a gift.

In life, there are adventures. Dare them! Tears flow more frequently, sleep comes less easily, and you may begin to wonder why God does not seem to care, whether He is really listening or if God is even there at all. You find yourself without any resources or income. Overnight you have almost become a beggar. You feel like sinking into a depression. It is a time that no one understands you, not even your children or your relatives.

My Visits to Heaven and Hell

This is a point of testing. It is a time that can make a person either bitter or better. When some people reach this point, they simply accept defeat and give up. Others refuse to allow the tough times to defeat them and persevere to overcome their difficulties.

What can you do when all hope seems lost? Why do some people manage to turn their problems into opportunities and impossibilities into possibilities? The ultimate measure of a man is not where he stands in moments of comfort and convenience but where he stands at the time of challenge and controversy. The world will pay for courage and persistence and nothing else.

Hidden Greatness

You must decide what you want, when you want it and what you need to know and do to get it. You must also know Who you need to know to help you get it. Your motivation must also be pure. You should not be pursuing a goal in order to get back at somebody and make him/her feel bad. The goal must be worthwhile, not flaky. Goals must be balanced.

It doesn't pay to succeed in the workplace or home and neglect your relatives, parents and friends. Balance is a key to success in life. Goals must be purified through the filter of God's Word. As we read His Word and pray about our goals, clarity begins to come into our operations. The Bible says:

Elizabeth Saidimu

Commit thy way unto the L̲o̲r̲d̲; trust also in him; and he shall bring it to pass. Psalm 37:5

This book of the law shall not depart out of thy mouth; but thou shalt meditate therein day and night, that thou mayest observe to do according to all that is written therein: for then thou shalt make thy way prosperous, and then thou shalt have good success. Joshua 1:8

Success means the achievement of a desired aim. Success will stabilize and sustain you through your greatest accomplishments and your bitterest adversities. If you remain focused in the midst of adversities, you will realize that what appears to be a permanent obstacle in the way of your attainment of your dreams is only a figment of your imagination.

Have you wondered why so many men and women work so hard and honestly without ever achieving anything in particular or why others do not work hard at all and yet get everything? The Bible says:

For I know the thoughts that I think toward you, saith the L̲o̲r̲d̲, thoughts of peace, and not of evil, to give you an expected end. Jeremiah 29:11

Seeds of Greatness

There is a seed of greatness created and hidden within you. It awaits you to arouse it, water it, weed it and thereafter it will just grow. Successful people have formed the habits of doing those things that most people do not want to do. Good and bad habits ape, tiny daily choices that accumulate. It is like a child who grows a little each day.

It is said that necessity is the mother of invention. Sometimes the challenges that come our way could be blessings in disguise. People often run away from challenges rather than deal with them. It is through facing such challenges that you will discover hidden strengths and skills you never knew you had.

Start looking at your challenges from a different perspective because out of every challenge there is a blessing. Behind every giant there is a Promised Land flowing with milk and honey. Do not let your focus be on the giant, but on the promise.

You may be faced with difficulties and lack, but through that experience the Lord will teach you to trust in Him and maximize the little that you have. Your situation provides an opportunity for you to see the divine provision and intervention of God.

When the apostle Paul was put in prison for preaching the Gospel, he turned that trial into an opportunity to write part of the New Testament. His time spent in prison influenced more lives than when he was preaching from city to city in the eastern terrains. His prison epistles are even now influencing millions of Christians. Turn your challenges into blessing, and you will discover amazing treasures.

What Do Others See in You?

Others may see gifts and special talents in you that you might not see yourself. It does not take long before your family, friends or mentors notice the hidden treasure in you. Often the talent becomes obvious when a person can do a task with ease and enjoyment, while other seems to strain to perform the same task. You may never know how good you are until someone tells you.

The apostle Paul saw the hidden gift in Timothy, his spiritual son, and admonished him to stir up the gift within him (see 2 Timothy 1:6). Timothy become a preacher of the Gospel and was very instrumental in the ministry of Paul.

It is my prayer that you will find these three key valuable, as you pursue to discover the hidden treasure in yourself. Once you discover these treasures, I will teach you in my next article how to nurture those treasures to fruition so that they do not remain dormant.

He that goeth forth and weepeth, bearing precious seed, shall doubtless come again with rejoicing, bringing his sheaves with him.   Psalm 126:6

In order to grow, start exercising the gift of God deposited in you so that you can maximize the potential He has given you. God has given you this moment,

My Visits to Heaven and Hell

and it is yours to maximize. So stop bickering and murmuring about frustration and look for ways to get double for your trouble. God wants you to start going fishing and bringing in a double harvest. When we talk about maximizing the moment, we mean maximizing your relationships.

Message No. 11

Tithing, Other Giving and Stewardship

We Are Stewards of God's Resources

Every believer is a steward of everything he possesses:

> *As every man hath received the gift, even so minister the same one to another, as good stewards of the manifold grace of God.* 1 Peter 4:10

> *Moreover it is required in stewards, that a man be found faithful.* 1 Corinthians 4:2

A steward is one who manages, administers and takes care of that which belongs to someone else. Since God is the One who gives every material blessing, we acknowledge His ownership.

> *For all things come of thee, and of thine own have we given thee.* 1 Chronicles 29:14

> *Every good gift and every perfect gift is from above, and cometh down from the Father of lights.*
> James 1:17

My Visits to Heaven and Hell

God asks us to tithe, and His purpose for tithing is seen in the Old Testament. Tithing is a privilege, and it expresses faith.

Tithing comes with God's special promise. Learn to be a generous, cheerful giver. God asks us to tithe from what He has given, and a tithe means 10%.

> *And all the tithe of the land, whether of the seed of the land, or of the fruit of the tress, is the LORD's: it is holy unto the LORD.* Leviticus 27:30

> *Thou shalt truly tithe all the increase of thy seed, that the field bringeth forth year by year.*
> Deuteronomy 14:22

Jesus commended tithing:

> *For ye tithe ... [this] ought ye to have done.*
> Luke 11:42

God's purpose for tithing, as seen in the Old Testament, was two-fold: 1) To support the poor and needy, and 2) To support the Levites.

To Support the Poor and Needy

Among the Israelites, the harvests of every Sabbath year (every seventh year) was reserved for the poor.

> *But the seventh year thou shalt let it rest and lie still; that the poor of thy people may eat: and what they*

leave the beasts of the field shall eat. In like manner thou shalt deal with thy vineyard, and with thy oliveyard. Exodus 23:11

For the poor shall never cease out of the land: therefore I command thee, saying, Thou shalt open thine hand wide unto thy brother, to thy poor, and to thy needy, in thy land. Deuteronomy 15:11

And thou shalt not glean thy vineyard, neither shalt thou gather every grape of thy vineyard; thou shalt leave them for the poor and stranger: I am the LORD your God. Leviticus 19:10

To Support the Levites

The Lord required a special "third-year" tithe for the Levites, the orphans, the widows and the aliens:

At the end of three years thou shalt bring forth all the tithe of thine increase the same year ... And the Levite, (because he hath no part nor inheritance with thee,) and the stranger, and the fatherless, and the widow, which are within thy gates, shall come, and shall eat and be satisfied; that the LORD thy God may bless thee in all the work of thine hand which thou doest. Deuteronomy 14:28-29

To those who give God makes a special promise:

> *Give, and it shall be given unto you; good measure, pressed down, and shaken together, and running over, shall men give into your bosom. For with the same measure that ye mete withal it shall be measured to you again.*   Luke 6:38

This passage teaches us that we control the flow (amount) of God's blessings and provision to our needs. If we give spoonfuls to the Lord, He will pick up the same spoon we use and use it to spoon out what we have asked Him for. If we have faith to give shovelfuls to the Lord, He will pick up the same shovel and use it to shovel back to us what we need, a much more abundant blessing. When we have the least amount of money, the Lord is teaching us to double our tithe, giving 20% of our limited amount of money to the Lord.

God does what He says. If we give, it will be given back to us in proportion to our giving.

Tithing is a privilege

Several centuries before the law was given on Mount Sinai, Abraham gave a tithe (a tenth of his increase) to a representative of God (see Genesis 14:18-24 and Hebrews 7:1-2). Jacob promised to give a tenth of all that God blessed him with (see Genesis 28:22). Jesus said that we shall not neglect the tithe (see Matthew 23:23). Hence giving and tithing should not be understood as Old Testament laws or a religious obligation. Rather this is a privilege for those who choose to exercise their faith to give.

Tithing Expresses Faith

Tithing and giving offering does not buy God's blessings, but it does release blessings upon our lives (see Malachi 3:10). Those who tithe are expressing their faith in God in the most practical way possible. They are saying, "I believe that the 90% that I have left after tithing, has God's blessing on it. And with God's blessing on the 90%, I can purchase more than the 100% would have without His blessing."

It takes faith to believe this. God's Old Testament people tithed, not only their money, but also their crops and herds — oil, wine, flour, fruit, wood, animals — and any other possessions.

Be a Generous and Cheerful Giver

The Bible teachers us that we are to give willingly and cheerfully, from a spirit of generosity (see Exodus 25:2 and 2 Corinthians 9:6-7). God does not measure our giving by the amount we give. He rewards is according to what is left after we have given. Jesus said that a tiny amount given by a widow was greater than all the others because it was *"all ... she had"* (Luke 21:4). Generous giving is proof of our love, faith and maturity (see 2 Corinthians 9:11-12).

The poor need to give because they need God's blessings to break the curse of poverty (see 2 Corinthians 8:2). Jesus Christ, our ultimate example, became poor in order to bless us (see 2 Corinthians 8:9). To refuse to be a faithful steward by giving is an act of robbery and rebellion toward God (see Malachi 3:8-12). To yield to His purpose in giving is to receive an "open heaven" and abundant blessing and protection from want and famine.

Message No. 12

God's Nature Is to Bless

When we seek God's blessing as the ultimate value in life, we are throwing ourselves entirely into the river of His will, power and purpose for us all. Our other needs become secondary, when we are really immersed in what God is trying to do in us, through us and around us for His glory.

Let me tell you that, as guaranteed by-product of sincerely seeking blessing, your life will become marked by miracles. How do I know this? Because He promises it, and you have seen it happen in your own life.

God's power to accomplish great things suddenly finds no obstruction in you. You are moving in His direction. You are praying for exactly what God desires. Suddenly the unhindered forces of Heaven can begin to accomplish His perfect will through you, and you will be the first one to notice it.

What if you discovered that God had in mind to send you twenty-three specific blessings today, but you received only one of them? What do you suppose the reason would be?

Ask, and it shall be given you; seek, and ye shall find; knock, and it shall be opened unto you.
Matthew 7:7

My Visits to Heaven and Hell

Ye lust, and have not: ye kill, and desire to have, and cannot obtain: ye fight and war, yet ye have not, because ye ask not. Ye ask, and receive not, because ye ask amiss, that ye may consume it upon your lusts.

James 4:2-3

Even though there is no limit to God's goodness, if you did not ask Him for a blessing yesterday, you did not get all that you were supposed to get today. If you do not ask for a certain blessing, you forfeit others and receive only those that come to you only when you ask. In the same way that a father is honored to have a child beg for his blessing, your father is delighted in what you covet most.

Perhaps you think that your name is just another word for pain or trouble or that the legacy you have been handed from your family circumstances is nothing but a liability. You just do not feel like a candidate for blessing. There are Christians who think that once you are saved, God's blessing sort of drizzles over your life at a predetermined rate, no matter what you do, no extra effort required.

If this is true, then you have slipped into a ledger-keeping mindset with God concerning your blessing account. You have a column for deposits and one for withdrawals. If God has been unusually kind to you lately, then you may think that you should not expect much more. Consequently, you will not ask Him to credit your account. You might even think that He should ignore you for a while or even debit your account by sending some trouble your way. This kind of thinking is sin and a trap from the devil.

When Moses said to God on Mount Sinai, *"Show me your glory"* (Exodus 33:18-23 and 34:6-17), he was asking for a more intimate understanding of God. In response, God described Himself as *"the LORD God, merciful and gracious, longsuffering, and abundant in goodness and truth"* (Exodus 34:6). How incredible! The very nature of God is for us to have goodness in so much abundance that it will overflow in our unworthy lives. If you think about God in any other way than that, I am asking you to change the way you think.

Blessings Are Not Like Sneezing.

You are at a spiritual retreat in the mountains with others who want to experience a fuller Christian life. For the duration of the retreat, everyone has been matched with a mentor. Yours is in her seventies, and she has been touching lives for God longer than you've been alive. She has just knelt down to pray. You can't resist listening to what she will pray for and to know how she starts her prayer.

How exactly does a giant of faith begin her prayer? You wonder, "Will she pray for revival? Will she pray for the hungry around the world? Will she pray for the suffering?"

When she begins her prayer, you are surprised to hear her saying, "O Lord, I beg You, first and foremost this morning, please open my way. Please bless me and rescuer my life from all troubles which come from Satan."

Great men and women of faith think differently than the rest of us. Is it possible that God wants you to be selfish in your prayers, that He wants you to ask for more and more? I have met many earnest Christians who take it as a sign of immaturity to think such thoughts. They assume that they will seem impolite or greedy if they ask God for too many blessings.

Do you think like that? I want to show you that such a prayer is not the self-centered act it might appear, but, instead, a supremely spiritual one and exactly the kind of request our Father longs to hear.

> *The blessing of the L<small>ORD</small>, it maketh rich, and he addeth no sorrow with it.*   Proverbs 10:22

Why not make it a lifelong commitment to ask God every day to bless you? God's nature is to bless, and through a simple, believing prayer you can change your future. You can even change what happens one minute from now.

Message No. 13

Every Member Is a Minister

Every Member Is a Minister

God's people are not to be like little children, always looking to others for help. They are to grow in Christ, that they might serve in the Kingdom of God. The Jewish believers had this same problem in early New Testament times:

> *For when for the time ye ought to be teachers, ye have need that one teach you again which be the first principles of the oracles of God; and are become such as have need of milk, and not of strong meat. For every one that useth milk is unskilful in the word of righteousness: for he is a babe. But strong meat belongeth to them that are of full age, even those who by reason of use have their senses exercised to discern both good and evil.*   Hebrews 5:12-14

Every member is to become a ministering member, one who ministers to the Lord, to other believers and also to unbelievers.

Serving and Help

This refers to practical service in the local fellowship. It would include the office of deacon, but it takes in many other activities as well.

Exhortation (To Encourage)

To exhort means "to encourage, inspire, warn and inform" the people of God. The purpose of this ministry is to stir up believers to worship, work, war and witness for the Lord. The exhorter puts fire in our faith.

Giving

This ministry involves the giving of one's earthly goods (usually money) for the support of God's work. The giver must be honest, sincere and humble. He must be sensitive to the Spirit and gifted with wisdom. Only then can his giving be to the right people, at the right time, for the right reasons.

Administration

This ministry refers to wise, strong, loving leaders who know how to plan, organize, train and establish budgets and accountability in the church. It involves the structure and organization needed to oversee the affairs of the church (see Acts 6:3).

Mercy

This ministry requires sympathy, a caring feeling for others and wisdom to know what to do. Wisdom is linked with practical action. It is a calling which not only meets practical needs, but brings faith, hope and love to those needing help. There is a great need in the Body of Christ for coaching glad angels of mercy (see James 2:13-17).

Miracles and Healing

Miracles show God's power and prove His presence. Their purpose is to point unbelievers to God and build up the faith of the saints. They are signs of divine love in action for those in need. These ministries prepare the way for God's Gospel of grace. The gifts of healing (plural in the original Greek manuscripts) are to provide Christ's healing power to those who are sick. What a blessed thing to have these gifts working in the lives of the members of the church and in its leaders!

More Ministries in the Body of Christ

- Intercession
- Hospitality (prayer and fasting on behalf of others has always been powerful).
- Visitation (We can take God's love to others when they can't come to us).
- Social Concerns (How much God wants to reach the poor and needy, those who have been put out and put down!)
- Literature/narrative.
- Modern media
- Fine arts
- Reconciliation

The Conclusion

It is easy to see that many of the above ministries overlap or work together. A single person may have more than one function in his service for the Lord. Moreover, one ministry may become the foundation upon which another builds. All of us have a calling in the Body of Christ.

We begin where we are, with what we now have, and the Holy Spirit, our Divine Helper, will provide the fruit and gift which we need for our calling. It is our duty to cultivate or develop the fruit, by turning to God's Spirit during difficult times. And we must learn to excel or do well in the use of our spiritual gifts. Our desire is to become good and faithful servants of the Lord Jesus Christ.

Personal ministry is best discovered and developed within the fellowship of a local Spirit–filled church. Under wise and loving leadership, we will find our place and function in the Family of God. In this way, the Church of Jesus Christ will become strong and sound. Then we will be ready to minister to the Lord, to one another, and to the whole wide world.

In witnessing to the world, everyone will need to understand:
- The plan — what will be done
- The purpose — why it will be done
- The procedure — how it will be done
- The people — who will do it

- The place — where it will be done
- The program — when it will be done

Jesus told His disciples that at the end of the age, the world would face a time of great distress and difficulty. Fear, hatred and greed would cause the nations of the world to war against one another. The *"last days"* will be dark days indeed (see Matthew 24 and Luke 21).

For, behold, the darkness shall cover the earth, and gross darkness the people: but the LORD shall arise upon thee, and his glory shall be seen upon thee.
Isaiah 60:2

There is a bright hope, however, for the Christian. When the darkness increases, the glory of God upon His people increase also (see Isaiah 2:17-18, 21 and Acts 2:17-18, 21). This teaches us that more people will hear the Gospel and be saved in the last dark, but glory–filled, hours than at any other time in history. This will be a great end-time revival. The light of the Gospel will shine into the darkness of a dying world.

God always brings a warning and a witness before times of great judgment (see Revelation 2:16). For this reason, He desires to unify the Church in her worship, work, warfare and witness. Revival will come only as Christ's power and glory are revealed through His Church throughout the world (see John 17:20-21 and Matthew 24:24). Wake up and let us serve the Lord with what He has given us. God bless you!

Message No. 14

The Heavenly Network

The godly network system consists of angels, believers and some people on God's mind and His wishes. One will remember that angels are: *"ministering spirits, sent forth to minister for them who shall be heirs of salvation"* (Hebrews 1:14). They are put into families and operate in different and specific ways, according to the family they belong to.

The Godhead knows the divine link that exists between the angelic families and their working systems. When Daniel prayed, an answer came from Heaven, but it was hindered in getting to Daniel because one of the angels carrying the message was arrested. It took God connecting in the heavenly with another family of angels to carry on the network. This was an archangel know as Michael, a fighter or warrior, sent to finish the prince of Persia. The portion related to this event reads:

> Then said he unto me, Fear not, Daniel: for from the first day that thou didst set thine heart to understand, and to chasten thyself before thy God, thy words were heard, and I am come for thy words. But the prince of the kingdom of Persia withstood me one and twenty days: but, lo, Michael, one of the chief

princes, came to help me; and I remained there with the kings of Persia. Daniel 10:12-13

Michael, a chief angel, was contacted and sent abruptly to minister to Daniel for the release of the message carried by Gabriel (a chief angelic messenger). This is how the traffic of angels is taking place in the heavenlies. When believers are praying or crying to God, He is there to send some angels in one direction or another. They meet on their way, busy doing what they are sent to do.

The godly, angelic network becomes strong, as believers become involved in it. When one individual makes a step toward knowing God, he/she enters in a networking system made up of the Godhead, angelic beings and believers. The way it works is that heavenly angelic beings are always at guard to get God's instructions on behalf of believers.

When a believer prays, he/she never commands the angel to do something for him/her, but God has the final decision to release, on behalf of one of the saints, angels that are needed at a time for the specific situation. Sometimes it does not take prayer, but God's sovereign work to intervene for His people.

Abraham was sovereignly visited by angels, but also he prayed to see Sodom and Gomorrah delivered (see Genesis 18:1-33). Lot and his family were saved (except his wife) because of Abraham's intercession.

The heavenly network is a spiritual matter that involves a human heart.

The Spirit- or Heart-Led Believer's Network

Believers may network at a natural level in various ways. God comes into such a networking system by touching someone to do a specific task for Him or on behalf of another believer. For instance, a believer who is awakened at night to pray for a fellow brother or sister or a group of people. This is called a Spirit- or heart-led network.

God touches believers and gives them visions or dreams to alert or instruct another member of the Body of Christ on some particular issue or even an outsider. With the conversion of Saul, Ananias was instructed by God to help the feared man who had just met the Lord and gotten saved. Ananias did not disobey, but did what he had been requested to do (see Acts 9:1-19).

A Spirit- or heart-led network works even with some who do not know God. They will have a dream or vision or hear God's voice or in some other way, receive God's instructions for a specific situation. One example would be the case of King Cyrus, who received instructions to build a house for the God of Israel (see 2 Chronicles 36:22-23). His heart was moved to fulfil the long-awaited prophecy of Jeremiah.

My Visits to Heaven and Hell

Nebuchadnezzar, a pagan king acknowledged that the God of Israel was the God of Heaven and had made him what he ultimately became. No wonder God called Nebuchadnezzar his servant, since he networked with Him to correct the Israelites. This confirms the writing that says, *"The king's heart is in the hand of the L*ORD*, as the rivers of water: he turneth it whithersoever he will"* (Proverbs 21:1).

It is important to note that although the Spirit- or heart-led network is effective in Christian circles, it also works to some extent in the spirit or heart of some people with a specific God-led assignment. In fact, the devil has even developed a certain networking for his selfish motives.

A Prayer

Lord Jesus Christ, I thank You that You are faithful, and You have promised to give me everything I need for life and godliness. Thank You for showing me that by serving money I'm really serving Satan. I affirm to You right now that You alone are my God. I choose to trust You for all my needs. I know You will provide them all, if I will serve you with my money.

Lord, I trust You for the strength and grace I'm going to need to keep this commitment to the will of God. Thank You for these steps toward true financial freedom.

The Great Commission

Through Mark 16:15, every believer is commissioned and called. Paul wrote to Timothy:

Who hath saved us, and called us with an holy calling ... according to his own purpose and grace.
2 Timothy 1:9

Every believer has a responsibility. The Great Commission to go and the Holy Calling to witness and serve are every believer's God-given authority to minister. Each one of us has three priestly ministries:

1. To minister to the Lord in prayer, praise and worship
2. To minister to one another in loving relational, financial and spiritual support
3. To minister to the world (unbelievers) by healing the physically and emotionally sick, casting out demons and telling them the Good News that Christ died for our sins, according to the Scriptures (see 1 Corinthians 15:3- 4).

When believers are taught how to fulfil these three ministries, many will assume their God-given privileges and responsibilities and say, like Isaiah, *"Here am I; send me"* (Isaiah 6:8).

My Visits to Heaven and Hell

Christ left us no privilege greater than to announce the Gospel to every creature. This is what the early Christian did day and night. They healed the sick, cast out demons and shared the Gospel from house to house, at markets, village wells, on the busy roadways and streets, in meeting places, from jail cells and in dungeons — anywhere and everywhere. They had no cathedrals or elaborate church buildings to inhibit their unbridled joy of ministry and sharing with those who were anxiously waiting to receive Christ. They went out where the sinners were and spread the Gospel. And we should live and breathe for one purpose only: to share the Gospel with the greatest number of people possible and by every means possible.

You do not have to be an ordained minister to share the Gospel. This is the privilege of every believer. Christians do not need a special call to do things Christ authorized them to do throughout the world. They only need to accept the honor conferred upon them of becoming an ambassador for Christ.

Every Believer Is Commissioned

Because every believer is commissioned and called, no special call is needed to be a soulwinner. Jesus' instructions are clear: *"Let your light ... shine before men"* (Matthew 5:16) *"Go out into the highways and hedges, and compel them to come in, that my house may be filled"* (Luke 14:23). He said, *"Preach the gospel to every creature"* (Mark 16:15).

If one nation is 88% Christian, while another is 88% non-Christian, our choice should be to reach the non-Christian nation. If a small field of ripened grain had a hundred reapers at work, while larger fields had only one reaper, which field would you toil in to save the grain? You should choose the field where the need is greatest and where there are fewest laborers to meet the need. If ten people were lifting a log, nine on the small end and one on the large end, it should not be difficult to choose where you should lift.

God Will Guide

As you motivate your members to pray for and go to the places that needs the Gospel, God's Spirit will begin to give guidance as they go. You cannot guide a ship that is stopped in the water. Movement is needed for the rudder to steer the ship, and so it is with God's guidance. Paul was en-route to Asia on a certain occasion (see Acts 16:6-9). This is the kind of guidance you may receive, if you stay sensitive and alert in your spirit (see Matthew 28:20 and 1 Corinthians 15:19).

Receive the Triple Anointing

God wants you to be a leader who gets results and makes an impact on your world. How can you be that kind of a leader? Leaders must align their lives with the standards of the Bible. This is where we start. We must handle money well, walk in humility and avoid moral compromise. But even with all that, we can still fail to be effective in our ministry.

Neither education nor special skills and abilities will give your ministry the power it must have to transform people's lives. What will? The full anointing of the Holy Spirit alone gives the heavenly unction you need to fulfill your function.

God has made us *"kings and priests unto God"* (Revelation 1:6). He wants us to have the power of kings and the purity of priests. We must experience His full anointing to have this. In this message, I will show you how the anointing will bring deliverance and strength and salvation to God's people.

Jesus introduced His ministry by proclaiming:

> *The Spirit of the Lord is upon me, because he hath anointed me to preach the gospel to the poor; he hath sent me to heal the brokenhearted, to preach deliverance to the captives, and recovering of sight to the blind, to set at liberty them that are bruised*
> .   Luke 4:18

He made it plain that it was because the Spirit of the Lord had anointed Him that He was able to have an effective ministry. The same rule applies to you and me.

Isaiah spoke of the power of the anointing in these words:

Elizabeth Saidimu

The yoke shall be destroyed because of the anointing.
                                        Isaiah 10:27

There is a beautiful chorus based on this verse. It says:

By the anointing, Jesus breaks the yoke,
By the Holy Spirit and power, just as the prophets spoke.
This is the day of latter rain.
God is moving in power again.
And the anointing will break the yoke.

Oh, it's true! We must have the Holy Spirit come upon us and impart a full anointing to lead God's people and fulfill the will of God in our generation. What is this anointing? What does the Bible have to say about it? How has it come upon leaders in past generations?

Three Types of Anointing

There are three types of anointing:
- The leper's anointing
- The priest's anointing
- The king's anointing

The Leper's Anointing

Leprosy was the most dreaded disease in ancient Palestine. This horrible condition slowly consumed the flesh of its helpless victims. Eventually the fingers, toes and other extremities would die, rot and fall off. Since the disease was contagious, the unfortunate leper was banned from his community.

To prevent others from coming too close, a leper was required to cry out wherever he went, "Unclean! Unclean!" The victim of this disease could only expect a slow, painful and premature death. Leprosy is a picture of sin, a graphic object lesson, by which the Holy Spirit dramatically portrays the consuming, horrible effect of sin on a person's life. Leprosy reveals sin and Satan's true nature. Leprosy, like Satan and sin, will steal our life, and eventually kill us and destroy our ministry.

The Law of Cleansing

One wonders why Moses laid down such elaborate rules for the cleansing of the lepers and his restoration. After these rules were made, there is not one case of an Israelite being healed of leprosy in all the Old Testament. Why would God have Moses lay down these rules then? It can only be for the reason that God placed a hidden or spiritual lesson in these rules He wanted us to learn. Let us examine the details of such rules (see Leviticus 14).

The rules which were prescribed by Moses to declare the leper clean and cured are an Old Testament picture of the New Testament cleansing from sin through Jesus Christ. All the elements of our salvation experience are there:

1. The shedding and application of blood, which portrays Jesus Christ shedding His blood to bear away and pay the penalty for our sin
2. Repentance and confession, which portray what we must do to be justified or be declared righteous, when we are born again
3. Running water, picturing water baptism
4. The leper's anointing with oil, which typifies the work of the Holy Spirit in our salvation experience

Therefore, as portrayed in the rules for the cleansing of lepers, when we believe in Jesus, we should:

1. Repent, turn away from our sin and rebellion and turn toward God and obey His Word
2. Confess our sins to God and received His forgiveness. If we do this sincerely from our hearts, we are saved (healed) from sin.
3. Be baptized in water. Next we are to obey Jesus Christ by being baptized in water.
4. Receive the anointing of the Holy Spirit. We experience this anointing bearing witness with our spirit that we are God's children (see Romans 8:16).

Anointing with Oil

To anoint means to put oil on or consecrate by applying oil. This was done after the leper had been saved and had obeyed the rules for cleansing. He now presented himself to the Levitical priest to be anointed with oil.

Oil is an Old Testament symbol of the Holy Spirit, and anointing a person with oil pictures the Holy Spirit coming upon him for a specific, designated purpose.

A leper, one defiled by the dreaded leprosy, when delivered and cleansed from its affects was then anointed with oil to show that he has been fully restored and ready to resume his place as a member of the family of Israel. Every sinner experiences the leper's anointing, when he is born again of the Spirit (see John 3:5-6). All who believe in Jesus and submit the way they live to His Lordship experience a measure of the anointing oil of the Holy Spirit (see Romans 8:9). These scriptures confirm that no one can be truly born again without experiencing some measure of the work of the Holy Spirit.

There is a fuller anointing, when we are baptized in the Holy Spirit, which we will discuss in more detail later under the subtitle The King's Anointing. This anointing is distinct from the primary work of salvation. Both, however, involve the work and ministry of the Holy Spirit.

The Three Areas of Life Affected (see Leviticus 14:14-18)

It is important to note that the blood of sacrifice and the anointing oil were placed on the ear, hand and foot. This shows us that our salvation and anointing experience (our healing from the leprosy of sin) affect three important areas of our life:

1. Our hearing the Lord's voice (our ears)
2. Our service for our Savior (our hands)
3. Our walk with Him (our feet)

If we do not hear God's voice, our service will not be fulfilling. We need the blood to cleanse our hearing, our service and our walk. We need the Holy Spirit's anointing to hear, to serve and to walk as we should. Both the blood of Jesus Christ and the anointing of the Holy Spirit are necessary parts of our *"great salvation"* (Hebrews 2:3).

The Sacrifice of a Spotless Lamb

Aaron and his sons entered the door of Moses' tabernacle and stood at the brazen altar. There they shed the blood of a spotless, blemish-free lamb, as a sin offering. By this, they experienced forgiveness from the penalty of sin, which is death (see Romans 6:23). This corresponds to being born again, or justification.

An Anointing to Holiness

Concerning the use of the holy anointing oil, God said:

And thou shalt anoint the tabernacle of the congregation therewith, and the ark of the testimony, and the table and all his vessels, and the candlestick and his vessels, and the altar of incense, and the altar of burnt offering with all his vessels, and the laver and his foot. And thou shalt sanctify them, that they may be most holy: whatsoever toucheth them shall be holy. Exodus 30:26-29

It is clear from this verse that whatever the holy anointing oil touched was holy. Once Moses poured this holy oil on the head of Aaron and his sons, they were then holy to the Lord.

This was an anointing to holiness, being set, apart to God for His service by right living and right behavior. Thus, the priestly anointing teaches us commitment to righteous and holy living, after we've been born again. From that time on, all priests were anointed unto holiness in the same way, set apart to the Lord (see Revelation 1:6 and 1 Peter 2:9).

Purity and Power

We must be saved, not only from sin's penalty and guilt, but also from sin's defilement, force and habit in our lives (see Matthew 1:21). Some preachers say, "We are saved *in* sin," but the Bible says that we are saved *from* sin. We are saved not to sin!

We are not saved to make a practice of sinning (see 1 John 3:8). Oh, how we need this priestly anointing to holiness!

God, we plead for You to pour it out on us in a limitless measure.

If we are not to be destroyed by His power at work in us, we must have His purity expressed through us.

The Three Anointings Speak of:
a) Justification — our being forgiven
b) Sanctification — purity of heart.
c) Authority and power

God wants us to enjoy the fruit of all three anointing in our lives and ministries. Now, let us examine some men in the Bible who enjoyed this "triple anointing" or "full anointing."

Examples

1. Melchizedek

Thou hast the dew of thy youth. ... Thou art a priest for ever after the order of Melchizedek.
                                          Psalm 110:3-4

Under the Mosaic order, one had to be a member of the tribe of Levi to be a priest. When Jesus came, He was born into the tribe of Judah, the tribe the kings were to come from (see Genesis 49:8-10). What right, then, did Jesus (or, for that matter, you and I) have to part of a priestly ministry? He was of the wrong tribe. The apostle Paul solved this dilemma in his epistle to the Hebrews. There he explained Jesus' priestly order (see Hebrews 7).

Melchizedek is one of the most mysterious characters in biblical literature. His name in Hebrews means "king of righteousness." He was also the king of a city known as Salem (later named Jerusalem, which in Hebrew means "city of peace").

So by translation, Melchizedek was king of peace and king of righteousness. He was the priest of the Most High God who blessed Abraham after his defeat of the kings. Abraham even gave him a tithe of the spoils of war (see Genesis 14:18-20). So, Melchizedek functioned as prophet, priest and king. As such, he was a fitting type or prophetic picture of the coming king, Jesus.

What made Melchizedek a prophet, a priest and a king? It was the anointing that was upon him. He functioned in the unction. God made Melchizedek who he was by anointing him. This is also the way that Jesus, the High Priest of our confession, operates, and this is the authority through which every Spirit-filled man of God operates. We exercise prophetic, priestly and kingly rights, only by virtue of the anointing.

2. Moses

Moses was another man who enjoyed this triple anointing. God used him to deliver His people from

Egypt. Then, also through Moses, God gave Israel the Law. Moses ruled over the Israelites for forty years, but he could do so only because he bore a very special anointing of prophet, priest and king.

As a priest, Moses interceded for Israel, and, as a kind, he ruled over them. A tremendous anointing for prayer and power characterized his life. He bore a full anointing. He was a man who exercised priestly rights of access to the Lord, as well as great kingly authority over the people. Interestingly, Moses was never given the title of priest or king, but he functioned in both of these capacities.

3. The Judges

The judges who ruled Israel on the other side of Jordan were men and women who also bore this triple anointing.

I need to clear up misconception about these judges. They were saviors in that they saved the nation from its adversaries. They were deliverers in that they delivered Israel from oppressive enemies. They were judges only in the sense that they brought their judgment and wise counsel to the day-to-day needs of the people. They were not judges in the sense of sitting on judicial thrones in court rooms handing down legal decrees.

After Moses died, Joshua and the judges (deliverers) who succeeded him bore the triple anointing to both deliver Israel from her enemies and to bring her back to spiritual renewal in their relationship with God. They would often function as priests, bringing the people back to God and God back to the people. They functioned as kings by raising up and leading armies that would throw off the yoke of oppressors.

These men and women led by righteous rule and decree, but they were never given the title of either priest or king. They just functioned in unction as both. As the Spirit of God came upon them during times of dire need in Israel, they would implement whatever actions God wanted them to take. This informal method of running things kept the leadership from becoming institutionalized and burdensome to the nation. Institutionalism has usually proven a curse to the common person whether in a nation or in the church.

4. Samuel

Samuel appears to be the last of this long list of men who bore the triple anointing for a thousand years. From Melchizedek to Samuel, God had put this triple anointing on men to provide leadership for His chosen people.

Like Moses, Joshua and the judges before him, Samuel was raised up by God for a special time of need in Israel. In keeping with precedent, he did not carry the title of priest or king. However, the function of a prophet, priest and king was evident in his life.

During the time when Israel needed to hear from the Lord, Samuel was anointed to prophesy. Because the Levitical priesthood had become corrupt, Samuel offered sacrifices and interceded for the people.

Samuel also provided the leadership Israel so desperately needed. Like Melchizedek, Moses and many of the judges, Samuel's ministry bore the indisputable power and authority of a king. He also functioned in priestly ministry, as he was anointed by God.

But this thousand years of godly rule was coming to an end. The winds of change were blowing strong in Israel. Discontent with God's way was underlying public opinion. The people would soon be demanding change that would have a dramatic impact on the way the anointing came upon men.

A Divided Anointing

Now, in effect, the anointing would be divided between men titled kings and others titled priests. The kings would be destroyed by their kingly anointing because of a lack of holiness, the Levitical priests would take the priestly anointing and prostitute it by the absence of authority and power in their lives.

An Anointing for Power Only
(see 1 Samuel 10:1)

Why was Saul rejected as king? It was because he grew impatient waiting for Samuel and intruded into the priest's office and offered sacrifices (see 1 Samuel 13:8-14). When Saul tried to function in that for which he had received no anointing, he was immediately judged and rejected. This illustrates the point. When Israel demanded a king, the anointing was divided. The king only had a partial anointing. No longer did Israel's leader have the prophet, priest and the king anointing. He only had the kingly anointing, the anointing for power, not the priestly anointing for ministry to God with obedience and holiness.

It wasn't God's will for Israel to have a king like the other nations. God's pattern for leadership had emerged through Melchizedek, Moses, Joshua, the judges and Samuel. God had been faithful to raise up leaders who bore his full anointing and judged Israel as both priest and king. But Israel chose, rather, to have a king like the other nations. They rejected God's theocratic rule, turning their backs on God as their King. And God gave them the desire of their hearts.

A true theocratic ruler bears God's full anointing. He rules as prophet, priest and king. But with Israel's choice of a king like the other nations, a man began to rule over God's people with a partial anointing. It was not restrained by holiness and good character. This dividing of the anointing had never been God's highest will for His people.

A Lack of Holiness Brings Failure

God knew that no man would ever be able to reign under a kingly anointing unless it was balanced by the priestly anointing for holiness to the Lord. Most of the kings of Israel and Judah failed in their leadership because of a lack of holiness in their lives. The Lord rejected Saul from being king for disobedience and intrusion into a ministry for which he had no anointing. And Saul ultimately took his own life.

David's reign was impaired by his immorality with Bathsheba, and Solomon's reign came to a disastrous end because of unholiness and idolatry.

Israel eventually seceded from Judah, and after about two hundred years, went into captivity, chiefly because of the sins of her unholy kings. Her kings bore the power of God's authority, but they didn't walk in His holiness. This brought a judgment of division on the nation, resulting in the dispersion of the Israelites to the ends of the earth. Thus, the most tragic era in Israel's painful history ended in ignominy and defeat.

Priests without Power

After the people had demanded a king, they began to experience a different kind of oppression. An emphasis on legalistic holiness devoid of God's power and authority had replaced the unselfish, merciful, loving leadership of men like Samuel. The Pharisees of Jesus day were the ultimate extension of this error. These partially anointed "priests without power" did not stand before God and plead for the people, as had Moses. When God threatened to annihilate Israel for her sin and disobedience, Moses' intercession had saved the nation (see Exodus 32:30-35).

Now, instead, the Pharisaical denomination, with all its sectarian pride and legalism, began to assume commanding influence over the religious life of the nation.

Legalistic Demands

The Pharisees demanded a strict adherence to the letter of the Law. At the same time, they lost sight of the purpose of the Law and grew totally insensitive to human need. This inflexible legalistic demand for adherence to non-biblical religious rules made them unmerciful, vengeful and arrogant. They lost sight of the fact that all men were sinners in need of God's mercy, and they heaped condemnation and death on anyone they could catch in the act of breaking any of the commandments.

This pushed them into hypocrisy unrivaled in religious history. Jesus directed His fiercest rebukes at these "teachers of the laws." They had invented laws they themselves wouldn't obey, and they condemned others for failing to obey them.

> *The scribes and the Pharisees sit in Moses' seat: all therefore whatsoever they bid you observe, that observe and do; but do not ye after their works: for they say, and do not. For they bind heavy burdens and grievous to be borne, and lay them on men's shoulders; but they themselves will not move them with one of their fingers. But all their works they*

do for to be seen of men: they make broad their phylacteries, and enlarge the borders of their garments, and love the uppermost rooms at feasts, and the chief seats in the synagogues, and greetings in the markets, and to be called of men, Rabbi, Rabbi.
Matthew 23:2-7

Someone well said, "The gap between what we say and what we do is the measure of our apostasy."

Spiritual Pride

The Pharisees "showy holiness" was compounded by their spiritual pride. Emphasizing holiness and biblical knowledge, without the power of God's Spirit in your life to make it work, is a grievous error. Paul warns us against religious leaders and denomination who have become ensnared by this failure (see 2 Timothy 3:2-5).

The failure of the kings who bore God's power without the priestly anointing for living holy lives brought God's preliminary judgments on Israel. The pharisaical priests carried a priestly anointing, but they were devoid of God's power. This produced a religious based on the outward appearance of holiness without an inward change of heart. This oppressive system brought God's final judgment on Israel. The nation had failed to accomplish God's purpose in the earth.

The Triple Anointing Restored

God's people had undergone great suffering at the hands of Israel's unrighteous kings. They had experienced God's judgment as a result of their leader's errors. Thus, God's promise brought great hope to them:

> *And I will restore thy judges as at the first, and thy counsellors as at the beginning: afterward thou shalt be called, The city of righteousness, the faithful city.*
> Isaiah 1:26

To a people, who for centuries had known only leadership with a partial anointing, this was a promise of glorious restoration. God promised to give them leaders again who would rule with the same anointing as their first judges — men like Moses, Joshua and Samuel. This recurrent theme was often part of Isaiah's message:

> *Behold, a king shall reign in righteousness, and princes shall rule in judgment. And a man shall be as an hiding place from the wind, and a covert from the tempest; as rivers of water in a dry place, as the shadow of a great rock in a weary land.*
> Isaiah 32:1-2

The identity of this righteous king unmistakably emerges as we read further in the Scriptures:

> *For unto us a child is born, unto us a son is given: and the government shall be upon his shoulder: and his name shall be called Wonderful, Counsellor, The mighty God, The everlasting Father, The Prince of Peace.*
>
> Isaiah 9:6

This Prince of Peace would also enjoy the prophetic, priestly and kingly anointing:

> *The LORD shall send the rod of thy strength out of Zion: rule thou in the midst of thine enemies.*
> *Thy people shall be willing in the day of thy power, in the beauties of holiness from the womb of the morning: thou hast the dew of thy youth.*
> *The LORD hath sworn, and will not repent, Thou art a priest for ever after the order of Melchizedek.*
>
> Psalm 110:2-4

He who was to come would bear the full anointing of God, being at once King, Prophet and Priest. He would bear a strong scepter and rule as a righteous king. He would be a *"priest for ever after the order of Melchizedek."* His anointing would be so great that He would become known as "The Anointed One" (Messiah in Hebrew and Christ in Greek).

God's Promise Fulfilled in Jesus

God's promise to restore the full anointing has been fulfilled in Jesus Christ. He was *"anointed ... with the oil of gladness above [His] fellows"* (Hebrews 1:9). Jesus rules as our great *"High Priest"* (Hebrews 3:1) and as *"Lord of lords and King of kings"* (Revelation 17:14). He alone bears *"all power ... in heaven and in earth"* (Matthew 28:18). He alone *"is made unto us wisdom, and righteousness, and sanctification, and redemption"* (1 Corinthians 1:30). Unity or harmony *"is like the precious ointment upon the head, that ran down upon the beard, even Aaron's beard: that went down to the skirts of his garments"* (Psalm 133:2). A beautiful illustration and truth is expressed in this verse. The anointing which came on the high priest ran from the head down over his body.

We Are to Bear His Anointing

We know that we are members of Christ's Body (see 1 Corinthians 12:27). We know that Jesus is the Head and High Priest (see Ephesians 1:22 and Hebrews 3:1). Hence, the "triple anointing" that was poured out on Him flows down to us, the members of His Body. We can partake of the same anointing that was upon Him.

His was the ultimate illustration of the anointing God wants us to have. As church leaders, we are to bear His anointing, an anointing to live righteous, holy lives and an anointing to heal the sick, cast out devils and preach this Good News of the Kingdom to the ends of the earth. In short, it is an anointing of power.

Peter said that we are *"a royal priesthood"* (kings and priests) (1 Peter 2:9). John the Revelator reported:

"And hast made us unto our God kings and priests" (Revelation 5:10).

Steps to Receiving the Triple Anointing

1. Be Born Again:

The first qualification necessary to be a candidate for the leper's anointing is that you must have received Jesus Christ as your Savior. If you are a child of God, then you may receive the leper's anointing, the first of the three anointings.

2. Be Baptized in Water:

If you haven't been baptized in water, take that next step. As you are being baptized, recognize that God wants to do a supernatural work in your heart. Expect any lingering sinful habits or besetting sins to be broken as you are *"buried with him by baptism"* (Romans 6:4).

> *Knowing this, that our old man is crucified with him, that the body of sin might be destroyed, that henceforth we should not serve sin. For he that is dead is freed from sin.* Romans 6:6-7

In a scriptural water baptism, you can receive your priestly anointing, to walk a new life, free from sin's domination. Expect it to happen as you are immersed in the waters of baptism.

Be Baptized in the Holy Spirit

Your kingly anointing for authority and power comes from Jesus Christ. John tells us, *"The anointing which ye have received of him abideth in you..."* (1 John 2:27). As already stated, it flows down from the head to the Body. John the Baptist said of Jesus: *"I indeed baptize you in water ... but he shall baptize you with the Holy Ghost, and with fire"* (Matthew 3:11). John implied that Jesus Christ would baptize the same way he had done, only He would do it in the Holy Spirit, instead of in the water.

Desire the Holy Spirit Baptism

How did John the Baptist baptize? The candidates came to him desiring water baptism, and you must come to Jesus, desiring the Holy Spirit baptism.

Let Jesus Do the Baptizing

The people who came to John allowed him to baptize them. They didn't try to baptize themselves. You must let Jesus baptize you in the Holy Spirit. On that first Day of Pentecost, the Spirit *"filled all the house where they were sitting"* (Acts 2:2). The fact that they were sitting, made it easy for Jesus to baptize them. They were not in some kind of frenetic, religious, hyperemotional state trying to baptize themselves.

Be Immersed in the Holy Spirit

When John baptized the people in water, they were immersed in the waters of the Jordan River. Jesus will baptize you in the Holy Spirit. He is the Baptizer, the Holy Spirit is the spiritual water, and Jesus will immerse you in it.

As at Pentecost, lift your voice in prayers and praises to Jesus, and receive the Holy Spirit's filling. Allow Him to give you a heavenly language, for prayer and praise to your heavenly Father. As the Spirit gives you words or syllables to say, speak them out in faith to God. You will not understand the words, but your heavenly Father will:

> *And they ... began to speak with other tongues, as the Spirit gave them utterance..*   Acts 2:4

Do the same thing right now!

With this baptism, the beginnings of your kingly anointing will commence. Then, as with all the other anointings of the Spirit, it will grow and increase as you go on walking with the Lord. Hallelujah!

What We Have Learned

Through this section we've learned that God wants to train us to wait on Him and hear His voice. We've been taught how to view trouble as His instrument of refining. We've learned to avoid the traps of pride, sexual sin and the love of money. We've come to understand that those whom He calls must be refined and trained by the Holy Spirit in the school of tests and trials. The greater your responsibility, the more intense His dealings with you will be.

We Need the Full Anointing

However, if we have learned all of these things but fail to lead God's people with the full anointing we see in Jesus Christ, it is all for nought. Without God's Spirit anointing our ministry, we cannot effectively evangelize, teach, preach, work deliverance or healing or do the *"greater works"* promised us as church leaders (John 14:12). All we do will be the result of the energy of the flesh, with no lasting fruits.

It is most important that church leaders walk in holiness and depend on the Spirit's power. Lasting spiritual power can only be found in a holy life, and all who walk in holiness may have God's power in their life. We must experience both.

To emphasize the point: Any separated living, while devoid of God's power and yet neglect holiness puts us in the position where the anointing we carry will destroy us (see Matthew 7:21-23).

John tells us:

> *The anointing which ye have received of him abideth in you ... . As the same anointing teacheth you of all things, and is truth ... , even as it hath taught you, ye shall abide in him. And now, little children, abide in him; that when he shall appear, we may have confidence, and not be ashamed before him at his coming.*   1 John 2:27-28

Elizabeth Saidimu

This word *abideth* seems to be the key:

Abide in me, and I in you. As the branch cannot bear fruit of itself, except it abide in the vine; no more can ye, except ye abide in me. I am the vine, ye are the branches: He that abideth in me, and I in him, the same bringeth forth much fruit: for without me ye can do nothing. If a man abide not in me, he is cast forth as a branch, and is withered; and men gather them, and cast them into the fire, and they are burned. If ye abide in me, and my words abide in you, ye shall ask what ye will, and it shall be done unto you John 15:4-7

Abide in Jesus! How do we best lead with full anointing? By abiding in Jesus. *Abide* means "to remain, continue; stay; to have one's abode; dwell; reside." Paul said it this way:

As ye have therefore received Christ Jesus the Lord, so walk ye in him: rooted and built up in him, and stablished in the faith, as ye have been taught, abounding therein with thanksgiving.
Colossians 2:6-7

Independence and self-sufficiency are mature virtues, but they can be harmful in our spiritual relationship with Jesus Christ. He says, "Abide!" In other words, remain in Me! Depend on Me! For the branch to abide in the vine means that it stays connected. It thus keeps the life of the vine flowing into it. Its fruitfulness depends on this vital connection to the vine.

In this same way, we must remain in a close, vital relationship with our Lord Jesus Christ. If we do, His life, His anointing will ever flow to us and through us. Let us be like Mary, who chose to sit at His feet and hear His words (see Luke 10:38-42). Then we will minister out of a full anointing of Jesus Christ's kingly and priestly office. Worship and praise will become our very breath, and we will be equipped with His power and gifts to free others into the same liberty.

How deceptive it is and how tragic for a man upon whom God has laid His hand to take the anointing and use it for his own purposes. Don't do it! Always be a Jesus-pleaser!

Chapter Eight
Called To Full-Time Ministry

All of this was happening while I was still in full-time employment. I had been a banker for twenty-eight years when the Lord called me to full-time ministry. This did not come as a surprise to me. He had asked me if I would be willing to do a job of cleaning His children some years before, and my answer had been, "Yes." The process took many years, but all through those years, He kept reminding me periodically of what we had agreed upon.

Three years before asking me to resign, He told me that He would change my job. Then, a year before I left, He told me that some changes would take place at my work place. He said that when I would see those changes, it would be my time to move. The changes took place, and I knew the time had come. Then God gave me the date and details of what was to happen.

My last day of employment as a banker would be the 28th of February of that year. He told me that there were more bankers than ministers of the Gospel.

Before this, the Lord had given me a ministry which He said should be called "Women of Worship." It was based on the book of Esther chapter 5. Here is a quote from His actual words:

My Visits to Heaven and Hell

This ministry is based on the book of Esther, chapter 5. This is going to be the beginning of a big mission.

On the 28th of February, when I left the office I had called home for twenty-eight years, I did not know what to do next. I went home, and when I got to my living room, I sat down and said to the Lord, "Lord, here I am."

This might sound easy, but I can tell you that it was not. I had to leave a well-paying job, to come home and converse with Jesus. This was seen as madness by a number of my friends and even some of my family members. My human resource manager was on my case. He asked me to reconsider my decision. Humanly speaking, he was right, as were all the other people who tried to talking me out of my call.

My manager was thinking about the fact that I had a mortgage and now I was going home to nothing. He wanted to know if I had a Plan B. But I'm sure that all of those who have been called by God will agree with me that when He calls, there is no Plan B. God's plan is always A, A, and A. Amen!

One day, during my last week at work, I was on my way to the bank. Many people had already talked to me, asking me to re-think my decision about leaving my employment. Aside from the mortgage, I had four children to raise, all of them in school. It would have been logical to re-consider my decision. I talked to the Lord that morning and said, "Lord, tell me. Is it really You who has called me."

I was not asking this because I did not know that He was the One who had called me, but just to be doubly sure. It's never easy to make such a decision. Even the men of the Bible had plenty of excuses.

This is what He said to me, and He said it loud and clear: "I called the twelve (see Luke 9:1, 2), I sent the seventy (see Luke 10:1-2), I am now sending you, and I will send others as well." From that day forward, I never again asked God about His call on my life. It didn't matter what anyone said.

Just about two and a half months after I had resigned, the Lord sent someone from the United States of America, to bring God's anointing to me.

Enter Jeanette Biggers

Jeannette was the servant God send to me to bring His anointing. She came all the way from the United States. After she had left Kenya, Jeanette wrote her testimony and e-mailed it to me. Here is an excerpt from that testimony:

> I hope that as you read this report on my trip to the nation of Kenya, it will catapult you into a new place with the Lord. It is very important that right up front I make perfectly clear to you that this story is not really about me, but about the goodness of our loving Lord.

My Visits to Heaven and Hell

When I think back on the many events that happened (especially the third day I was there), I see myself as the donkey that carried Jesus into Jerusalem on Palm Sunday. The donkey would have been very foolish to think the shouts of joy and hosannas were for or about him. Nonetheless, what an awesome privilege to be a spectator and watch what the Lord did during the twenty-three days I was gone!

This trip was full of firsts for me. First time I went to Africa. First time I was sent by myself. First time I didn't know what I was supposed to do when I got there, nor know for sure where I would spend the first night.

First time the entire trip was not paid for in advance. First time I was so tormented by thoughts of possible sexual attacks, diseases or death. These were not unwarranted thoughts, as the fear factors were real, if you looked at the official warnings that were given me when I got the yellow fever inoculation.

But I don't resent those days of fog-and-molasses-type thinking because the Lord used all of the above to take me to a new level of commitment. Something like when Abraham was told to sacrifice his son, Isaac. A few weeks before I left, I told Curtis (my husband), "I have to go, but I don't have to come back." I wasn't trying to be overly-dramatic. It was that this mandate from Heaven was so strong I had to go, even if I returned in a body bag!

Perhaps I should also mention that it was the first time that nine days before I left, I had less than $10 in my ministry account and over $2,000 on the credit card for plane tickets, shots, etc. Plus, no other money for even food, let alone a place to stay or transportation while there.

For me, this whole Kenya trip started July the fifth of 2010, when Gabriel, our friend from Kenya, told us about his upcoming August 5th 2011 trip to return to his village to have a groundbreaking service/dedication for a Bible college.

As Gabriel talked, I heard the Lord speaking to me and saying, "You have a deposit, to deposit into Kenya." It was only eight words long, and yet it was as if the nation of Kenya had been placed inside of me, and this year [2011], I started to call it my Kenyan baby.

I did not get to go with Gabriel the previous year, and then began an unusual time of desperation. So many times over the months I have wept over the nation and my inability to get there. Yet I told someone that, even if I had $5,000, I could not go until the Lord told me to do it. Little did I know how much timing was a key

My Visits to Heaven and Hell

part of this whole story. In March of 2011 the Lord started letting me know exactly what to do and when. I was glad that finally I was headed toward Kenya!

When my visa did not arrive in time for my May 2nd departure date, I knew that it was of the Lord, even though I didn't know the reason and it cost extra to change my ticket. Only during the first two weeks I was in Kenya did I understand it all had to do with timing and the Lord getting my heart in line with His heart.

A month before I left for Kenya, I met by e-mail an American lady who lives in Eldoret, Kenya, and she extended an invitation for me to stay at her house while I was in the country. Sounded good to me, but in the next few days I felt that she was part of the plan, but knew that I was not supposed to go there first.

Five days before I flew out I received another gracious offer from a Pastor Peter, a Kenyan I met last year in Ashland, Virginia. He offered to drive from Kitale to Nairobi airport, and I could stay with him and his family.

He has twelve churches in Kenya and assured me there were ministry opportunities. However, within two days the Lord let me know that this was not where I should go first either. Hmmm... Now what, Lord?"

Elizabeth Saidimu

Eight days before I flew out I woke up having less than $10 for the entire trip. However, that day I had $175 put in my hand, and two days before I left, I had another $450 given to me. That $625 looked really good, and Father used it to bless many people in Kenya and get me bottled water, etc, in Kitale. I was also blessed with the loan of a Kenyan phone. This really was a wonderful gift to both Curtis and me, as it eased his mind just to hear my voice daily.

In the airports and on the planes, people would ask me where I was going, and when I told them Kenya, they wanted to know what I was going to do there. It was hard to reply, "I don't know."

"Where are you going to stay?"

"I don't know. "

All I knew was that had a deposit to deposit into Kenya, but no idea of what it was or where I was supposed to end up in that nation.

Hopefully these details are not too boring, but to understand the magnificence of it all, sometimes you need to see the behind-the-scenes facts.

When I arrived in Nairobi, my luggage didn't. As I stood there about 10:30 at night filling in paper work, I remember that the Lord had not allowed me to be picked up by Pastor Peter. You see, Kitale is about a seven-hour drive from

My Visits to Heaven and Hell

Nairobi. If I had listened to common sense and let him meet me, it could have turned into a great inconvenience for him. God's timing was already at work.

Gabriel's sister Jackie was waiting for me at the airport, along with Elizabeth Saidimu. I had never had any communication with either one of these ladies. Gabriel had asked Jackie to find a "reasonably priced" place for me to stay. Having not been able to find one, she called Paschalia, a friend of hers, to ask if she knew of a "reasonable priced" place. Best I can figure, this call was made less than thirty-six hours before I boarded the plane. The friend had just happened to have insisted on seeing Elizabeth's newly-remodeled hostel less than twenty hours before Jackie called her. The hostel is like a rooming house for university students. Elizabeth had rented it the first part of April and felt a great urgency to remodel it quickly and had just done so when she mentioned it to her friend and then Jackie called her.

Up to that point Jackie and Elizabeth did not know each other. The friend gave Jackie Elizabeth's phone number, and because she thought I was coming on Monday morning, they agreed to meet on Sunday afternoon.

Elizabeth asked her husband if it would be all right for me to stay at their home, if I chose to do that. Robert asked her, "Do you know this lady?"

Elizabeth Saidimu

"No," she answered, "but Jackie is looking for a place for her."

"Do you know Jackie?"

"No."

He replied that it would be all right for me to stay there if I wanted. How amazing for him to be willing for a complete stranger to stay in his home.

Elizabeth later stated that she didn't know what would be a reasonable price to charge a lady minister from America, and so she e-mailed her cousin in America and asked her. Although her cousin is usually very quick to answer her e-mails, this time she ignored her and didn't answer until the second day I was in the country. Since Kenyan time is seven hours ahead of us, I was about eight hours from my departure time when Elizabeth met Jackie at the hostel.

Elizabeth picked up Jackie and was at the airport about 8 AM on May 16th, only to wait a couple hours without any planes arriving. Elizabeth asked Jackie if she knew the flight number. Since Jackie didn't, she suggested she call her brother and ask.

Gabriel let Jackie know my arrival times was after 8 PM not 8 AM. Jackie then told him that Elizabeth was there with her, and would he like to speak to her. Since Elizabeth hadn't heard

My Visits to Heaven and Hell

back from her cousin, she asked Gabriel, "What is your idea of a reasonable price?" To which he had the audacity to tell this complete stranger, "My idea of reasonable price is FREE!

Elizabeth later testified that up to that time she had been thinking how much she could charge me for transportation, accommodations, etc. But the moment he said, "Free," she knew I was her assignment and that she was to take care of me at no charge. All of these small details were worked out by our heavenly Father, without any of my input or help.

Elizabeth's home is thirty minutes from Nairobi City. I had been well informed about the dangers of Nairobi in the daytime, let alone after dark, but let me tell you what the Lord did for this little girl of His. He had me in a place that, according to someone else, is where politicians and millionaires live. It was a double-gated community with security guards at each gate, plus barbed wire and an electric fence around the complex! I don't think our President is any safer than I was. Did I need all that to be safe? Of course not, but it is just soooo amusing and amazing to me the way the Lord worked that out.

For the entire time I was in Nairobi, my new friend Elizabeth treated me like royalty and watched over me like a mother would. So much so that I call her my Kenyan mom (and, yes, my own mother is fine with that).

For the first two days there, Elizabeth and myself shared miracle stories back and forth. Before I left my room on the third day, the Lord told me to pray a prayer of impartation for Elizabeth. I knew what that meant and that it was different from the normal prayers we had been having together. When I came out of my room, she shared that the Lord had given her a vision. The following is an excerpt from an e-mail she sent me.

You also remember the deposit you made on the morning of May 19, 2011. It was about 5 AM, when I woke up to spend some time with my Father. While seated in my living room, I had a vision and saw you rolling toward me a huge gold stone about the size of a normal room. As I stood and put my hands in front of me to receive the gold stone from you, the Lord showed me a short-handled spade or trowel. He suddenly spoke and said, "When someone comes to you for something, use the trowel that I have given you. Scoop it into the gold substance and give it to them." He also said that any time I scooped out the gold it would grow back by the time I made the next scoop.

My Visits to Heaven and Hell

He then told me, "My child, you have been faithful for a long time! You have been faithful with little! I have now lifted you, and I have given you more anointing. This anointing is from Me to you, to take to the world. You will scoop it to my people that will come to you. The anointing will take care of all the needs of My children, whatsoever the need will be, including healing, salvation, provisions – name it – it is contained there." The Lord left after speaking these words.

You remember the details of what we shared and the amount of time we spent with the Lord that day? We could not even leave the house because of the powerful anointing that was there. Remember what you shared with me about the visions you had in 1999 concerning the gold and it representing the anointing? That was also the same year that I was healed of cancer.

We may never get to know how long He had planned all the details leading up to this day. But I now know beyond any doubt, because of the miracles that have taken place since the time you made the deposit, there has been a special anointing in my house from that day.

About ten days after I left Kenya, Elizabeth called me and, with reverence, said, "This anointing is something else." She then shared with me what happened in her native village when she returned home for a visit. Again I quote from her e-mail:

The last morning, my daughter came to call me from my bedroom and told me that I had visitors in the living room. This was the same day that we were traveling back to Nairobi, and we already had our bags in the car. I had just gone back to the room to ensure that I had not left anything that I needed to take with me.

There was no time to see visitors, but you know what? The car got a flat tire immediately, and that required it to be taken to the shopping center for fixing. This gave me time to see my uninvited guests. When I entered my living room I found a man that I had prayed with the previous day and a lady with a little baby, maybe about five months old. My dear, there was such a presence of powers of darkness in my house, my hair was standing on end. I trust that you understand these expressions.

The woman was staring at me without winking. There was a lot of tension. I knew there was work to be done. Remember the Lord had told me that there was a woman with needs? She was one of the reasons that I had not graduated, if not the only reason.

My Visits to Heaven and Hell

I greeted them, and the man started talking. He told me that this was his sister and that she did not have a sound mind. She was insane. He requested her not to speak, as she has always done. He gave me her story in brief because he knew that I was being waited for.

As I listened to the short story, I kept my eyes on the lady, who was staring at me, and the demons left her. I did not cast out any demons from her that day. They simply left as I stood and listened to her story from her big brother.

By the time I opened my mouth to speak with her, she was free. The presence of the Lord was evident in the room. Not only was she set free, but she also gave her heart to the Lord that day!

This lady being set free without Elizabeth doing anything reminds me of the book of Acts, when people were healed as Peter walked past them (see Acts 5:15).

Two weeks later she talked to the brother, and his sister is still well and doing fine. Thank You, Lord, for fruit that remains!

On the eighth day, I left Nairobi and traveled to Kitale, where I stayed with Pastor Peter and his wife Ann. Many wonderful things could be said about this couple, their ministry and all that happened in the next seven days.

As I close this testimony of God's timing, goodness and love, I want to tell this last detail about His provision for me while I was in this Third-world nation. As I stood at the airport, with over $2,000 in credit card debt waiting for me, I was handed an envelope. When I opened it up, it contained $1,860, which was more than 125,000 shillings in Kenyan currency! Also, when I returned, I had two love gifts waiting for me. So on the third day back, I sat down and paid off in full the ticket, shots and other trip essentials.

To God be all the glory!

Praise God!

I am so pleased to have finished the assignment which the Lord gave me, that of ensuring that I put this information into a book.

May God bless you.
Elizabeth Saidimu

Ministry Contacts

The author is available for teaching in seminars, workshops, conferences, Bible schools/colleges and churches, as well as other learning institutions. She is ready to answer questions regarding this book and also give explanations in detail as needed.

She has received over six hundred short messages from the Lord and is currently putting them together for your reading.

Write her at:

Elizabeth Saidimu
P. O. Box 61081-00200
Nairobi, Kenya

E-mail her at:*emsaidimu@yahoo.co.uk*

You may also follow her on twitter:*@esaidimu* and FaceBook: *Elizabeth Saidimu*
Call her at: *+254 722 305 630*

My Visits to Heaven and Hell

Elizabeth Saidimu for Heaven Light Ministries
Founder and Vision Bearer

Partners May Address Their Contribution

ELIZABETH SAIDIMU P.O. Box 61080-00200
Nairobi, Kenya. Cell: +254- 72 305 630.
Email: emsaidimuyahoo.co.uk
A/C No: 01111040000300 COOP BANK.
BRANCH: CO-OP HOUSE
SWIFT CODE: KCOOKENYA
MPESA ACC: 0722 305 630

"Those who will partner with me in bringing up these children, I the Lord will partner with them in all that they do," thus says the Lord.

www.ingramcontent.com/pod-product-compliance
Lightning Source LLC
Chambersburg PA
CBHW071307110426
42743CB00042B/1211